Even mature believers tend to think of Heaven as the beautiful, perfect place with gold-paved streets they'll reach at the end of their lives. But isn't Heaven so much more than that? How should it impact our everyday interactions and relationships? In *Kingdom Come*, Pastor Jimmy Witcher makes simple and accessible the idea that the Kingdom of Heaven should not be a far-off concept, but part of our everyday lives. This is countercultural—but Pastor Jimmy shows us how to deepen our relationships with God and others and invite Heaven down while we are still on Earth.

MARK DRISCOLL
Founding and Senior Pastor of The Trinity Church
Author of Spirit-Filled Jesus

The Bible talks a lot about God's Kingdom. What is it? Where is it? Can we experience it now? Pastor Jimmy Witcher asks and answers those questions and many others in *Kingdom Come*. I recommend this book to everyone who wants to know God and experience His abiding presence actively working in their lives. You will walk away with refreshing insight on God's love and work in our generation!

TOM LANE
Apostolic Senior Pastor
Gateway Church

Pastor Jimmy Witcher is an amazing leader who is passionate about seeing the Kingdom of God advance in our generation. *Kingdom Come* is full of practical insights that will help you shake off religion and lay hold of the significant life you are called to in Christ.

JORI BUCHENAU
Senior Pastor
Grace Thru Faith Church

In a world of chaos, confusion, and busyness, even believers find themselves wondering if the abundant Christian life is just a fairy tale. The "normal" Christian life looks a lot like the lives of everyone else trudging through the day. But what if overflowing peace, victory, and joy were not only possible for us, but were always intended to be our norm? What if we were meant to walk through every day feeling fully alive in God's presence? In *Kingdom Come*, Pastor Jimmy Witcher presents a compelling case that experiencing Heaven on Earth is exactly what God intended all along, and gives us practical instruction on how we can begin to live this reality today. Right now. In the midst of any circumstance. If you desire all that God has for you in this life, I challenge you to read this book and allow it to redefine your "normal."

D. MARK ALLEN
Senior Pastor
Life Fellowship

We all desire to be known, to matter, and to make a difference. In *Kingdom Come,* Pastor Jimmy Witcher shows how we can fulfill those longings of the human heart in our lives, and reveals that the Kingdom of God is not in our distant future, but something we can experience today! When Jesus declared "the kingdom is at hand," He forever altered what we should believe is possible in this world. This book contains deep truths unpacked in simple ways—as only Jimmy can do. As you read, I pray you are stirred to dream about Heaven and believe you can experience it in your life today.

———————————

AARON KENNEDY
Senior Pastor
Opendoor Church

KINGDOM COME

Living in Heaven on Earth

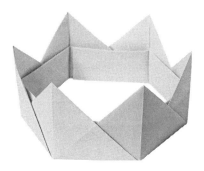

JIMMY WITCHER

Published in Amarillo, Texas, by Trinity Fellowship Church.

ISBN Paperback 978-1-7331281-0-0
ISBN Ebook 978-1-7331281-1-7

Printed in the United States of America

To my beloved children, Knox, Jas, and Blaze:
As I embarked upon this project, it became clear to me that you are
my real audience.
It was your faces I saw as I wrote, and it is my sincere hope and
prayer that these pages might help you in your own spiritual journeys.
May you see God the Father a bit more clearly every day.

ACKNOWLEDGMENTS

The process of writing this book has been a journey, and I am so thankful for all of those in my life who made it possible. To Kimberly, my beloved wife of over thirty years, thank you for your love, support, encouragement, and patience as I read, and re-read, the manuscript to you! I am who I am because of you and your investment in our "us." To my children, Knox, Jas, and Blaze, thank you for all your support and input all along the way. And to Knox, thank you for your incredible leadership! Without it, this would never have been completed—you truly have a gift! I'm thankful for Bree Proffitt and all your help and support bringing the work to completion. Thanks to Shannon Last for all of your instruction, editing, creative input, and expertise. Finally, I am thankful to the elders, pastors, and congregation of Trinity Fellowship Church. You are the most amazing people on Earth! It is a joy getting to serve you every day.

TABLE OF CONTENTS

FOREWORD

I've been colorblind all my life. I knew I had trouble distinguishing colors when I was growing up, but it wasn't until I was a young adult that a test confirmed that I am red-green colorblind. I didn't get a single question right—out of ten or twelve pages! For my entire adult life I have just had to concede that I don't see colors very well. Before leaving home, I always ask my wife if my clothes match because I don't trust myself. (I've learned that lesson the hard way when I've tried to get creative without checking with her!)

But about five years ago, someone mentioned the invention of glasses that correct color blindness in most people. They are called EnChroma; if you search YouTube you can see people weeping as they put the glasses on and behold colors for the first time. It is amazing!

When I first put mine on, a new world emerged that I had never seen before. What astounded me most was the beauty of the color green. It had always seemed a dirty shade of gray—I had never known that highway signs have such a bright and beautiful hue.

I also started noticing pastel colors I never knew existed—especially with cars on the road. I had no idea there were so many variations of colors and how subtle and attractive most of them they are. The first time I went to a professional baseball game with my new sunglasses on, I was stunned by the shades that popped from the stadium, the field, even the clothing of the fans around me. I felt like the man who had been born blind that we read about in the Gospel of John. Upon seeing him on the road, Jesus "spit on the ground, made mud with the saliva, and spread the mud over the blind man's eyes." When the man had rinsed out his eyes, "he came back seeing!"[1] After putting on my new glasses for the first time, I truly related to him: "I know this: I was blind, and now I can see!"[2]

You are about to have the same experience. By the time you close this book, you'll see the world around you through new eyes. Page by page and chapter by chapter, Pastor Jimmy Witcher explains scriptural truths that many of us have read before but didn't understand. Once you begin to read the Bible and to view—and live—your life through the lens of God's Kingdom, you will never be the same.

I know, because this happened to me. When I was younger in my faith, I had read about the Kingdom of God in the Bible many times. I'd prayed the Lord's Prayer, where we ask the Father to "Let your Kingdom come…" and also state at the end, "Yours is the Kingdom." But no matter how often I read God's Word or prayed the Our Father, I was blind to it. I couldn't see that God's Kingdom was present all around me and no idea how it impacted my life. The day I realized the truth about it was like the day I put on my colorblind glasses for the first time. I saw the world anew, and it changed my life forever.

This book will do the same for you: it will make the Kingdom of God visible and show you how to see, experience, and internalize it.

I have known Jimmy Witcher for over twenty-five years. After thirty years of leading Trinity Fellowship Church, I was looking for someone I could trust to lead the church after me. And with God's direction, I found the perfect person.

I can't say too many good things about Jimmy Witcher. He is one of the most gifted and intelligent people I know and his character is an example to all. Many times, I've seen incoming pastors become jealous and territorial, and run the former pastor off.

---

1 John 9:6-7 (NLT)
2 John 9:25 (NLT)

Jimmy is the opposite. He has treated me with incredible respect and has kept me as a part of the preaching team and the eldership of the church. His security is in the Lord—and it shows. He is a true Kingdom man!

Jimmy Witcher has a unique authority to write this book. He has done a masterful job of explaining the reality of God's Kingdom—and how we can practically experience it right now. He isn't just teaching out of his head. His wisdom comes from his life experience, his prayer, and above all, his relationship with Our Lord.

I trust and pray Our Lord will enlighten and bless you greatly as you read *Kingdom Come.*

———————

JIMMY EVANS
Senior Pastor
Gateway Church

Do you want to go to Heaven?

Growing up, it seemed to me that this was the central question of Christianity. The songs I sang talked about getting into Heaven. The sermons I listened to told me what to do to gain admission.

I also heard about the place I'd wind up if I didn't make the cut: Hell. Heaven, I believed, is where God lives, and Hell is where the Devil lives. It seemed to me these spiritual extremes were opposing forces who were perpetually grappling over humanity, pulling souls into their respective camps. I believed everyone's life had an expiration date, so we had better pick a team before our time is up. The focus was always on what happens after our life here ends.[3]

These eternal questions of Heaven and Hell, God and the Devil, good and evil are laced through all of our lives, no matter our path. Hardwired into the human psyche is the question every culture, tribe, nation, and individual has sought to answer: Where do we go when we die? As we struggle to define the meaning of life, we all sense there must be something more out there, a deeper reality just beyond our reach.

Sometimes the answer seems close by, just waiting for us to discover it. Other times, the cynic inside us wonders if life is really

---

3 Now don't freak out on me yet! You're just getting started. I'm setting you up for a "big point," not trying to trick you into judging yourself by wondering if you're good enough to get into Heaven. We'll cover that later. (And by the way, you're not good enough. Neither am I. No one is. It's why we need Jesus!)

just a crapshoot—a roll of the divine dice setting our brief existence in motion.[4]

For most of us, these philosophical questions about life's mysteries are deferred as we run off to work, to school, and out with friends. They go unanswered as we get married, raise kids, and get caught up in the busy pace of life. We're sure that Heaven is great and Hell is obviously bad. But right now, we tell ourselves, I don't have time to go into the weeds. I have things to do. I have a family to tend to, friends to hang out with, and bills to pay. I have challenges to overcome, a destiny to fulfill, and a desire to make a difference in the world here and now. So we leave these questions on the afterlife and eternity to the religious leaders, philosophers, and poets, and we focus our energies on simply getting through the day.

But what if we've got it backward? What if Heaven is something more than where we go when we die? What if we can experience it—even in part—right now? Now that would be something altogether different!

So let's ask: Did Jesus really come to earth, live His life, and die so that we could slide into Heaven at the end of things? If we are created from love and destined for love, then is the stretch of time between our birth and death meant to be merely endured? There's something more—isn't there? The answer is a resounding "YES!"

Jesus rarely spoke of Heaven in the context of our afterlife, but he spoke of the Kingdom of Heaven all the time! "The Kingdom of Heaven is at hand," he would say. "You are close to the Kingdom of Heaven," he assured us. "Our Father, who lives in heaven, your Kingdom come..." was His prayer.

So here's the point: The Kingdom of Heaven is not a state of mind. It's not a new way of looking at life. It's not some metaphysical

---

4 This is exactly what this book is here to address: What is that thing inside of us that hopes for more ... but expects less? Is it our hopes or our expectations that are out of whack?

mumbo-jumbo trying to trick you into believing that the challenges you face are not real. The Kingdom of Heaven existed before time and matter. It was modeled for us in the Garden of Eden when God created the earth. It was central to Jesus's life and teaching. And it's available to you right now!

The Kingdom of Heaven is a spiritual place that is accessible to you today. It has real ramifications on your day-to-day life. It is where our Heavenly Father lives. It is where we find His blessing, protection, and provision for every aspect of our lives. If we believe that Heaven and Hell are real possibilities, the stakes couldn't be higher. But our present life has a way of distracting us from eternal realities, which seem vague and far off.

I wrote this book for busy people in the midst of a busy life. It's not a theological treatise aimed at seminary students. It's for you to read as your life allows. You don't have to absorb it all at once. You can read a chapter with a latte[5] at your favorite coffee shop, on a lunch break, or in one of those all-too-brief and quiet moments when all the kids are finally tucked in bed.

First, we'll spend some time unpacking what I mean by "Kingdom of Heaven"—what it is, where it is, and how we can get to live there. We'll explore the power God gave us to choose our path. And we'll discuss the nature of God: His fatherly love for us, His desire to draw us near, and the radical promise He makes to us.

Then we'll explore some of the key things Jesus taught His disciples—and how those lessons are just as fresh and vital more than 2,000 years later. We'll talk about how God shapes every part of our lives, from our identity and purpose to our relationships and struggles. And we'll examine what it means to turn every aspect of

---

5 Or, if you're like me, a double short Americano with room (not cream, room)!

life over to God, to truly submit our will to His will—and why that makes all the difference.

That sounds pretty good so far, doesn't it? But nothing in life is that straightforward and easy. Everyone will face challenges; everyone will suffer. So I won't shy away from it in these pages. We'll face these realities head on: How do we live in the Kingdom of Heaven when we are in pain? How do we reconcile the injustice we see around us with the idea of a good, just, and loving God?

Jesus tells us to "keep turning away from your sins and come back to God, for Heaven's kingdom realm is now accessible."[6] He tells us that Heaven is a place where we can choose to live in this very moment—what an amazing promise! It's really good news: in fact, it is the Good News. Because of Jesus, we have direct access to the Kingdom of Heaven. Not only do we get to go there when we die, we also get to live there this very second and every second that follows!

Heaven has resources you need today. Heaven offers you protection. Heaven is real. Heaven is close. Heaven is available to you, right here, right now. Living in heaven means you will experience God's provision, protection, and purpose in the middle of your busy life. Jesus came to both make the way and show us the way into the Kingdom of Heaven. It would not be an overstatement to say he was obsessed with helping us find and live in the Kingdom of Heaven.

That's my goal, too. I hope you find in these pages the answers you're seeking, and lessons you can apply to your day-to-day life. After all, what does day-to-day life have to do with "getting into Heaven"? Everything! This is the primary message of Jesus's life on earth. Heaven is not merely where we go when we die: It is where

---

God the Father rules and reigns and offers His children love, care, direction, and fulfillment—here and now.

So let me ask you again: Do you want to go to Heaven? How would you answer if I told you that Heaven is waiting for you this very moment? What if you could experience Heaven without waiting until you die? Would you want to go? Would that possibility be worth exploring?

Jesus has already paid the price of admission for us. And through Jesus's death on the Cross, God threw open the door to His living room and invited us to come right in.[7] The Kingdom of Heaven is right here within our grasp. It's up to us to step through the door and make the choice to live there.

So I invite you on a journey to find Heaven. It's real, and it's closer than you think. If you seek His Kingdom, God promises you will find it, and so much more: right here, right now.

---

7 I mean this literally! He threw open the door. Matthew 27:51 tells us that when Jesus died on the cross, the veil in the temple was torn in two from top to bottom—like ripping a piece of paper. This veil separated what the Jews called the "Holy Place" from the rest of the temple. They believed God's very presence was in the Holy Place. By ripping the veil, God was showing that His presence was open to everyone through Jesus! Hebrews 10:19-22 tells us the same thing. So, stop reading this book and check these verses out. Really, it won't take you long. Download the YouVersion bible app. I like *The Passion Translation*.

CHAPTER ONE

The Kingdom of Heaven

"I am the Gateway. To enter through me is to experience life, freedom, and satisfaction. 10 A thief has only one thing in mind—he wants to steal, slaughter, and destroy. But I have come to give you everything in abundance, more than you expect—life in its fullness until you overflow!¹¹ I am the Good Shepherd who lays down my life as a sacrifice for the sheep."

~ John 10:9-11

Why on earth would Jesus give up His awesome gig in Heaven with God the Father and come to live among us as a man? He gives us a hint here in John 10. He came to be a gateway, a path, an opening. He came to lead His people to "good pastures" where they will find a "rich and satisfying life."

Over and over, throughout the Old Testament and the New Testament, the image of the shepherd appears. Abraham was a shepherd. So was Moses. So was David. It is to the humble shepherds, quietly keeping watch over their flocks at night, to whom the angel of God reveals the Good News of the birth of Jesus. Jesus is called the Lamb of God. In the Parable of the Lost Sheep, Jesus compares Himself to a shepherd who leaves ninety-nine sheep to go in search of a single sheep who strayed—and rejoices over the rescue of that one lost sheep.[8] After His death and resurrection, Jesus tells Peter his task on earth would be to "feed my lambs."[9]

8 Luke 15:1-7
9 John 21:15

Chances are you've never run across a shepherd—but in Jesus' day, shepherds were common and shepherding was essential work. To our modern minds, the comparison of the Son of God to a lowly, uneducated shepherd is astonishing. Sheep aren't very bright,[10] and they require constant tending. They have to be led to water, food, and shelter. Without a vigilant shepherd, they are easy prey for the native bears, wolves, and mountain lions that roamed the countryside. The shepherd places himself between those threats and the creatures he protects! Jesus takes that to the next level: He declares Himself to be the "good shepherd" willing to sacrifice His own life for His sheep. Imagine the Almighty giving it all up for the weak and vulnerable! But he does not stop there. In this text we find a nugget of truth that goes way beyond salvation.

Jesus does not just say that he came to provide a way for His sheep to survive and avoid the predators of life. Look again at John 10:10: "But I have come to give you everything in abundance, more than you expect—life in its fullness until you overflow!" The word Jesus uses, *perissós*, means over and above, superabundant, distinguished, excellent, better—so completely over-the-top as to seem wasteful! Jesus is painting a picture of Himself as the abundant provider and diligent protector of our lives.

David praises God in Psalm 23, saying, "1 The Lord is my best friend and my shepherd. I always have more than enough. 2 He offers a resting place for me in his luxurious love. He takes me to an oasis of peace, the quiet brook of bliss. That's where he restores and revives my life."

Jesus did not come so we could get to Heaven some day. He came to give us access to His "luxurious love." He came so that we

---

10 Now, this is not to say that you are not very bright. I'm sure you are brilliant! The truth is though, without Jesus guiding us, we all lose our way. The tentacles of selfishness pull us to away from the path. How often do we say to ourselves, "Why did I say that? Why did I do that? What's wrong with me?" It is our daily dependence on Jesus as our "good shepherd" that keeps us headed in the right direction.

might "experience life, freedom, and satisfaction" in every area of our lives! In other words, he is opening up the way for us to begin experiencing the benefits of Heaven right now.

Yet, Jesus also tells us, there is something else out there—the thief—whose only desire is to steal, kill, and destroy the lives of the sheep. What happens when a sheep separates from the flock and wanders away from its shepherd? It becomes vulnerable to attack. The Devil and his demons are real, and their only desire is to wreak havoc on our lives.

Our modern age exhorts us constantly to declare our independence and seek out untrodden paths. The expression "You do you" is ego disguised as individual freedom. Insisting on our autonomy keeps us out of the blessing of the Kingdom of God, no matter how hard the enemy tries to convince us otherwise. Counterintuitively, submitting to God—acknowledging Jesus as the shepherd of our lives—leads to true freedom. Step one to living in the Kingdom of God is acknowledging our dependence on Him.

In December 1996, I was a Young Life cabin leader at a high school ski trip in Silvercliff Ranch, Colorado. We would ski all day, then return to camp for dinner and "club"—fun skits, singing, and a short message about Jesus—and then discuss the message in small groups in our cabins. On the last night, everyone was encouraged to seek God for themselves. My only job as a counselor that night was to walk around the camp making sure everyone was okay.

I had grown up in a Christian family and personally decided to accept Jesus when I was seven or eight years old. I read my Bible, went to church, led the youth, and taught Sunday school classes. I tried to be "good" because I believed it was what God wanted. But, on that night, I came face-to-face with all my doubts. "Is this real? Is Jesus real? Do I even believe what I am selling here?"

The questions began to consume me. I just started walking along a path. The night was bitterly cold, as the Rockies in December often are, and the sky was perfectly clear. The view of the stars was breathtaking! Wrestling with my doubts and fears, I walked until the path ended at the base of the cliff and a thought entered my consciousness: "God, if you are real—if this is, if you are real—would you show me a shooting star?" My next thought came in an instant. "You don't test God." But with nothing to lose, I looked up.

Now, my view of the sky was mostly blocked by the cliff shining silver in the moonlight. Looking up, I could only see a sliver of black sky, but I perfectly remember what I saw. As soon as my eyes met the sky, a star shot from my left to my right parallel with the cliff edge! A bright beam of light, cutting through the darkness, traveling from horizon to horizon. I stood there speechless. God had heard my thoughts, and He responded.

In that moment, I knew God was real. I'd lived eighteen years believing it was true, but now I knew. I knew He cared. I knew He was personally and intimately involved in my life. I knew I could trust Him. I knew it was right to depend on Him. Something about the contrast of the vastness of the sky and mountains and cliffs and my own smallness really put things into perspective for me. That night, God literally moved Heaven—for me. I was forever changed by that encounter.

I felt a little like Mary's cousin Elizabeth must have felt, when she felt her infant (John the Baptist!) "jump and kick" in her womb as soon as he sensed Mary's approach. "And suddenly, Elizabeth was filled to overflowing with the Holy Spirit!" Overwhelmed, she says to Mary, "How did I deserve such a remarkable honor to have the mother of my Lord come and visit me?"[11]

My experience felt almost unbelievable. Yet the Bible is filled to the brim with stories of God revealing Himself not just to a sea of humanity, but to individuals—from Adam and Eve, to Noah, to Abraham, to Moses, and on down through the centuries. Sometimes He appears in person. Sometimes He comes in dreams. Sometimes it's just His voice from Heaven that can change the course of a life. Just ask Paul, who heard God's voice on the road to Damascus and was immediately converted from a Christian persecutor to a Christian witness and martyr. And of course, the details we know about Jesus's life show us without question how interested He was in the ordinary details of the ordinary lives of ordinary people.

Chapter 6 of the Gospel of Mark tells the story of Jesus multiplying five fish and two loaves of bread to feed more than five thousand hungry people. "By the time Jesus came ashore, a massive crowd was waiting. At the sight of them, his heart was filled with compassion, because they seemed like wandering sheep who had no shepherd. So he taught them many things."[12]

The scriptures also tell us about Nicodemus, a leader in the Jewish religious community, who came to Jesus one night. He recognized that God was clearly with Jesus. He had heard of the miracles and listened to Jesus teach. He wanted to know Jesus's secret to living with such blessing. Jesus got straight to the point in John 3:3. "Nicodemus, listen to this eternal truth: Before a person can perceive God's kingdom realm, they must first experience a rebirth." Jesus goes on to tell him, "Unless you are born of water and Spirit-wind, you will never enter God's kingdom realm. For the natural realm can only give birth to things that are natural, but the

---

11 Luke 1:41, 43
12 Mark 6:34

spiritual realm gives birth to supernatural life! ... For this is how much God loved the world—he gave his one and only, unique Son as a gift. So now everyone who believes in him will never perish but experience everlasting life."[13]

We're going to come back to this idea of "gift" a little later, in Chapter 7. For now, notice how Jesus is pointing Nicodemus to a spiritual place—translated at different points as "God's kingdom realm," the "Kingdom of God," "Heaven's Kingdom," and "Kingdom of Heaven." All of these point to the same place: Heaven, the realm of the Kingdom where God is the King.

Put simply, Jesus wants your life to be good. The Devil wants to destroy everything good. Listen to Jesus and follow His voice, and you find provision, protection, love, and care. Follow the voice of the thief[14] and you experience pain, grief, disappointment, and failure. This contrast sets the stage for how we often view the entire human experience: living in blessing versus living cursed, having abundant life versus barely getting by, finding fulfillment versus experiencing continual disappointment.

We all want the former. Yet we all experience the latter. The question is, do we have any real influence over how our lives play out?

Let's go back to the conversation between Jesus and Nicodemus. Jesus makes it clear that we have a lot of influence by connecting two concepts: entering the Kingdom of God and having everlasting life. For most of my Christian life, I understood this to mean, "Accept Jesus and you get to live forever in Heaven. Refuse Him and you perish in Hell." In other words, Heaven and Hell were juxtaposed, and my fate rested on a single decision: do I accept or reject Christ? While this view is not necessarily wrong, it is grossly

---

13 John 3:5-6, John 3:16
14 Which almost always sounds like our own voice, our own thoughts.

incomplete—not to mention misleading. It is quite possible to have the great reward of experiencing Heaven after you die, but miss out on fully experiencing the Kingdom of Heaven while you live.

Remember that in Luke 15, Jesus describes how the shepherd leaves his flock in search of "one lost lamb."[15] Toward the end of that chapter, Luke tells the Parable of the Loving Father, who rejoices when his wayward son comes home—because "he was lost but now he is found!"[16] It's not a coincidence that we see the word "lost" in both of these parables—because we can't truly be found until we recognize we are lost. Once we can see that, acknowledge that Jesus is our Savior, and entrust our lives to Him—we are saved. When Jesus proclaims the Kingdom of God, He calls all of us to a new life in Him.

This moment in a Christian's life is a dramatic event—but it's more than a one-time thing. It's also a lifelong process. The moment you first say "yes" to Christ is just the beginning of the journey! You chose Jesus in a split second, but living in the Kingdom of God means making a series of daily decisions to enter the gate Jesus shows us. It means saying "yes" over and over again throughout our lives.

Jesus says in John 3:15, "Those who truly believe in him will not perish but be given eternal life." This "eternal life" is not simply referring to what happens at the end of our physical existence. Eternal life is the doorway that Jesus is offering us to gain entry into the Kingdom of God and experience Heaven in the very present right now of every moment of every day.[17] Heaven is not just the place you go when you die: you can experience its blessings as you

---

15 Luke 15:5

16 Luke 15:31 (NLT)

17 "In some passages this zōé aiónios ... life, life eternal which is equivalent to the kingdom of God, and the entrance into life, means the entrance into the kingdom." Zodhiates, S. *The Complete Word Study Dictionary: New Testament* (electronic ed.). (Chattanooga, TN: AMG Publishers, 2000.)

possess eternal life right here, right now. You don't have to wait. You can hold it in your hands, wrap it around you, keep it, live in it, experience it. This is the Good News![18]

So, if eternal life is the blessing available to everyone who believes in and accepts Jesus, then what is the "Kingdom of God"?

Simply put, the Kingdom of God is the place where God rules and reigns. It is where he is in control, calls the shots, and makes the plans. It is the place where he engages with His children—offering blessings and providing loving correction where needed. It is where God the Father strengthens, empowers, and equips His children. It is the source of His provision and place of His protection.

The Kingdom of God is governed by God. There, His laws, principles, values, and truths reign supreme. All other pretenses of control fall away in the Kingdom. There's not even a hint of democracy. We have no say. Only His rule is allowed—and not because He is insecure, power hungry, or self-absorbed. Quite the opposite! He is a loving parent who knows our wants, needs, and desires better than we do. He knows where and when we need to be strengthened, encouraged, comforted, redirected, or chastened—just as he knows when we need to learn to persevere through a challenge to prepare us for some future opportunity. (We'll talk a lot more about this in Chapter 5.)

As Christians, we carry the Kingdom of God inside of us, but its boundaries don't stop there. If it were merely a state of mind or place in the heart, then Jesus would have said so. Let's look back at the beginning of John 3:2: "One night [Nicodemus] discreetly came to Jesus and said, 'Master, we know that you are a teacher from God, for no one performs the miracle signs that you do, unless God's power is with him.'" It was not the Kingdom of God inside Jesus that

---

18 In the Bible, the Greek word "gospel" literally means "The Good News."

attracted Nicodemus' attention. It was the effects of the Kingdom on those Jesus touched. And this isn't limited to Jesus—it's available to all of us.

The prophet Jeremiah said it this way in chapter 29: "11 'For I know the plans I have for you,' says the Lord. 'They are plans for good and not for disaster, to give you a future and a hope.'" Jeremiah was speaking to Israelites held captive by the Babylonians, telling them not to worry, because "God has you and he still has good plans for you!" His words ring just as true today, because God is unchanging. God still has us in His hands; He still has plans for us. That is what it is like to live in the Kingdom of God. It may not always be easy—in fact, we will often face difficult challenges. But we can know that He has a plan, it is for our good, and He will equip us with whatever we need to get through.

Psalm 100 reminds us once again that God is the Good Shepherd:
- *For he is our Creator and we belong to him.*
- *We are the sheep of his pasture.*
- *You can pass through his open gates with the password of praise.*
- *Come right into his presence with thanksgiving.*
- *Come bring your thank offering to him and affectionately bless his beautiful name!*
- *For the Lord is always good and ready to receive you.*
- *He's so loving that it will amaze you—so kind that it will astound you!*[19]

Look at that again. "[T]he Lord is always good and ready to receive you." Not in the distant future—now and always. So, the Kingdom of God is both spiritual and concrete. It's ahead of us, and with us right now, and in us. It is where we live eternally when we leave our earthly body behind, and a place we can choose to live in each and every day.

Remember what Jesus tells us in John 10: "I am the Gateway. To enter through me is to experience life, freedom, and satisfaction." Entering through Him takes us into the Kingdom of God. This is why Jesus left Heaven and came to earth. This is what Jesus told Nicodemus. And this is what he is telling us: the gate is open wide. The Lord is ready to receive you now and always. What's stopping you from walking through?

CHAPTER TWO

The Two Trees

Then the Lord God planted a garden in Eden in the east, and there he placed the man he had made. The Lord God made all sorts of trees grow up from the ground—trees that were beautiful and that produced delicious fruit. In the middle of the garden he placed the tree of life and the tree of the knowledge of good and evil...
~ Genesis 2:8,9

The Lord God placed the man in the Garden of Eden to tend and watch over it. But the Lord God warned him, "You may freely eat the fruit of every tree in the garden—except the tree of the knowledge of good and evil. If you eat its fruit, you are sure to die."
~ Genesis 2:15-17

The Garden of Eden was perfection itself. So, why did God make a beautiful paradise and then put a forbidden tree in the middle of it? The answer to this question tells us something about the nature of our Heavenly Father. Even more, it shapes and defines the purpose of our lives.

Let's go back to the beginning—the very beginning, before creation. One day God looked at His triune self—God the Father, Son, and Holy Spirit—and said, "You know what we need? More of us. More to love. More to relate with. A huge family!" And so it was decided. "'Let us make human beings in our image, to be like us. They will reign over the fish in the sea, the birds in the sky, the livestock, all the wild animals on the earth, and the small animals that scurry along the ground.'"[20] God created the universe, designed mankind, and put Adam and Eve in a perfect garden to be in relationship with one another and with Him, and to reign over creation.

Sounds like a King building His kingdom, doesn't it? A God so relational that the truest expression of His nature was to create mankind to receive His abundant love. But true love requires freedom—the opportunity to choose not to love (or not to be loved). Without the ability to choose, love is fake. It's hollow. It's a sham.

Forced love is not love at all. So the secret of the Two Trees is choice. The Tree of Life gives eternal life. The Tree of the Knowledge of Good and Evil brings death. And because God didn't design us to be robots, He gives us the liberty to decide which we want.

God has already chosen you. That's why He brought you into existence. God desires a real relationship with mankind—not in the universal but in the particular. He does not just love "us." He loves you! He is loving and kind. He is ready to shower His children with blessing, provision, protection, and empowering grace. God desires a relationship with every single individual He created. God desires a relationship with you and with me. All we have to do is choose Him.

I vividly remember the moment I was faced with this choice. I was seven, maybe eight years old, standing chest deep in the warm water of the church baptistery. The Reverend Roy Wheeler of Paramount Terrace Christian Church in Amarillo, Texas was standing next to me. I do not recall how I got to this place, but the moment itself is etched in my memory. To my right, I could look out the small window from the elevated tank into the sanctuary with its vaulted ceilings and rows of perfectly spaced pews. The bright stained glass windows were a stark contrast to the dark stained wood, yellow carpet, and orange seat cushions. I could see

---

my family looking up at me with an excitement and anticipation I did not, at the time, understand. I was more intrigued by seeing Reverend Roy wearing fishing waders under his baptismal cloak.

Then Reverend Roy asked me a simple question: "Jimmy, are you ready to make Jesus the Lord of your life?" I knew the answer was supposed to be a simple "yes," but I hesitated. I could sense this moment was a big deal. Was I ready? How would I know if I was ready or not? How did anyone know? The question ran through my mind. Was I ready to make Jesus Lord?

I loved Jesus. I knew He was alive, that He was good, and that He loved me. I got stumped on the word "Lord." What did it mean to make Him my Lord? Everyone was waiting, and I began to feel the pressure my hesitation was creating. So I blurted out a firm "yes." Reverend Roy put my hand over my nose and dipped me backward into the water.

I understand now that what I was sensing in the Baptistery that day was the awesome power of that choice. I said "yes" in that instant, but I have spent the rest of my life understanding what that "yes" means—making Jesus my Lord.

For many Americans, the idea of lordship is not only foreign, it's downright repulsive. After all, our nation was born out of a rebellion from the control of the British monarchy. We are an independent, pull-yourself-up-by-your-own-bootstraps kind of people. We love to celebrate the underdogs who achieve greatness against all odds through sheer force of will, discipline, and self-sacrifice. There is certainly nothing wrong with hard work, determination, and a clear vision. The problem lies with the spirit of independence.

If we pop the hood and look at what's powering our drive for independence, we find an ugly truth. It's not that we don't want others to see our success, it is that we want to get all the credit for it.

We want to earn the glory. We want to deserve it. We want success, and we want the recognition that success brings. In fact if we're honest with ourselves, we often desire the recognition even more than the tangible benefits of success!

This concept is foreign to God. God is Himself an interdependent being. He is one, and He is three—Father, Son, and Holy Spirit. His purpose for creation was relationship. His foundational view is driven by the concept of family, where success is not measured by individual achievement but by the collective experience of the whole. Ask any mother. While her heart genuinely celebrates each of her children's accomplishments, it is burdened for the one facing a challenge. This gives rise to the axiom, "A mother is only as happy as her least happy child."

In the Kingdom paradigm, we've got a King and his subjects; a father and his children. Here, success is not measured by personal achievement but by obedience. All opportunity comes from the King; thus, any and all success is credited to Him. So when we pursue success and recognition for its own sake, we block ourselves from accessing the full blessing and opportunity of God's Kingdom. This is not to say we won't go to Heaven when we die, but aspects of our life may very well experience Hell before we get there. Just ask Adam and Eve.

All they had to do to enjoy an eternity of blessing was choose to eat of the Tree of Life and stay away from the Tree of the Knowledge of Good and Evil. But what happened? The Devil showed up as a serpent and tempted Eve by telling her, "God knows that your eyes will be opened as soon as you eat [of the fruit from the Tree of the Knowledge of Good and Evil], and you will be like God, knowing both good and evil."[21]

It turns out that FOMO—what we call "fear of missing out"—has been around since the dawn of time. The Devil's ploy was to convince Adam and Eve that God was withholding something good from them. The great irony is that Adam and Eve were already "like God" because He created them that way. They weren't missing out on a thing—they were quite literally living in paradise. They were already experiencing everything "good." The only thing "missing," actually, was the knowledge of evil. And as he has done since time began, the Devil looked for a way to exploit their FOMO.

Genesis gives us insight into Eve's thinking in the moment: "The woman was convinced. She saw that the tree was beautiful and its fruit looked delicious, and she wanted the wisdom it would give her. So she took some of the fruit and ate it. Then she gave some to her husband, who was with her, and he ate it, too. At that moment their eyes were opened, and they suddenly felt shame at their nakedness."[22] So, what is the "wisdom" the Tree of the Knowledge of Good and Evil purports to provide? God's view. His seat. Total control. Complete independence.

Adam and Eve might have argued that being more like God meant having the ability to see both good and evil and only choose good. The problem is: who defines "good?" Follow the logic: if every individual can define for themselves what is "good" and what constitutes "truth," it creates a world of strife, envy, competition, and selfishness—which, in turn, introduces every kind of evil.

In the Kingdom of God, only He can define "good." Only a Creator who is outside of time, all-powerful, and all-knowing can see how the threads of our lives intertwine. Only He can determine the course of our lives that leads to real blessing, joy, and satisfaction. And we can help Him make that happen. When we choose to make Jesus the Lord of our lives, we step down from the throne of control over our own lives. We stop trying to define good and evil for ourselves, and choose instead to simply obey.

Submission is the key. Surrender is the path. Obedience is the way we discover our purpose.

I began to discover my purpose the moment I said "yes" to Reverend Roy's question, and let him dip my head underwater. Living in the Kingdom of God means learning to say "your will be done" countless times a day.

Each of us faces the same choice Adam and Eve faced. We can choose the Tree of Life or the Tree of the Knowledge of Good and Evil. We can choose obedience and interdependence or independence. We can choose God's way or our way. We can experience the blessings of living in the Kingdom of God or the pain of living outside it. We can enter in through the gate Jesus shows us, or stand on the other side, exposed, on our own.

Which will you choose?

CHAPTER THREE

Our Father

7 When you pray, there is no need to repeat empty phrases, praying like those who don't know God, for they expect God to hear them because of their many words. 8 There is no need to imitate them, since your Father already knows what you need before you ask him. 9 Pray like this: 'Our Father, dwelling in the heavenly realms, may the glory of your name be the center on which our lives turn. 10 Manifest your kingdom realm and cause your every purpose to be fulfilled on earth, just as it is fulfilled in heaven.

~ Matthew 6:7-10

Choosing to submit to our Heavenly Father's will lets us experience the blessings of daily life in the Kingdom of God. We know what the Kingdom of God is, but do we know the King? And do we understand what kind of relationship he wants to have with us?

It probably won't surprise you to know that Jesus provides this introduction and perspective! The paradigm of relationship that God chooses is that of a compassionate father caring for His beloved children.

Jesus wants to introduce you to His Father—who also happens to be God. Just as He is committed to proclaiming the Kingdom of God, Jesus wants us to recognize that God is not merely some powerful but distant deity. No, He is our Father, who lives in Heaven. Is Jesus really asking us to believe that the all-powerful, all-knowing, ever-present, outside-of-time God who spoke the entire universe into being wants to be...your Dad?

Like so many of God's mysteries, this can be hard for us to accept and understand. But this is no small point: Jesus personally uses the word "Father" over 220 times! It was a concept He worked diligently to drive into His disciples: God was not some distant and dispassionate deity. God did not live only between the pages of holy books. God was (and is!) a present, concerned, and involved parent who takes interest and delight in the day-to-day lives of His children.

Recently, I had the great privilege of officiating my eldest son's marriage. Standing three feet away, I led my son and his beloved through their vows, exchanging rings and sharing communion together. One of the most memorable parts of the ceremony came toward the end. They had each pre-recorded a short personal expression of their love and commitment. Standing there holding hands, they played those messages in front of all those gathered to celebrate the moment these two became one. It was magical!

In awe, I witnessed the whole world melt away until it was just the two of them standing there, in love, tears rolling down their cheeks, their voices expressing love, commitment, and excitement for a future that exclusively involved the other. That precious moment gave all of us a clear window into their devotion to one another and into the dynamics of their relationship.

As a dad and a pastor, it was one of the most special moments of my life. I was intensely aware of how God had allowed my wife and I to co-create our son, and to cooperate in His plan for the baby that had somehow grown into this kind, loving, principled man. I felt acutely how my children were my own flesh, but they were also children of God, beloved by their earthly dad and their Heavenly

Father. It was one of those moments where, for just a moment, I almost grasped the incredible mystery of the God who created us in His own image, and who wants to be our father and stand beside us at each juncture of life.

That's why Jesus hammers home the idea that God is not just His Father, but also ours! Teaching His disciples how to pray was not meant to be a rote religious exercise. Referring to God as "Father," and encouraging us to do the same, was a radical departure from the norm. It was a glimpse into His relationship with the Father. Jesus was demonstrating how He approached God, His view of God, and the dynamics that shape their interactions.

Most Jewish followers in Jesus's day viewed God from the standpoint of a penitent worshiper tentatively approaching the great I Am. Sacrifice and obedience were the core values that defined their relationship to God. The emphasis was on appeasing God's wrath and performing well enough to garner a bit of His favor and avoid punishment. We see this mindset in Jesus's own disciples. In John 9:2, they encounter a man who had been born blind. They ask Jesus, "Teacher, whose sin caused this guy's blindness, his own, or the sin of his parents?" Their immediate assumption was that someone had failed, and God had responded by punishing them.[23]

Just before He was arrested, and knowing what agony lay ahead of Him, Jesus prayed in anguish in the Garden of Gethsemane. "'Abba, Father,' he cried out, 'everything is possible for you. Please take this cup of suffering away from me. Yet I want your will to be done, not mine.'"[24] Here we see two key elements of the way Jesus taught us to pray: Jesus was experiencing the weight of our sins.

---

23 Jesus goes on to tell them in verse 3, "Neither. It happened to him so that you could watch him experience God's miracle." Jesus then heals the man using the encounter to teach his disciples about the light and darkness. His point was that you cannot truly see God (you are blind) if you keep looking at the relationship from a performance perspective.

24 Mark 14:36 (NLT)

So, he prayed: "Father, take this cup if you can!" But more than anything else, Jesus was committed to doing the Father's will: "Not my will, but yours be done! Your Kingdom come. Your will be done." Jesus was saying, "You are God, and I submit to your will!" Jesus lived out His submission to God even in the face of the greatest personal adversity.

True submission only happens when you choose to do what you are being asked to do when you don't want to do it. When you choose to bow to the authority you are under rather than press through with you own agenda, then you demonstrate true submission. Jesus exemplifies submission under the most extreme circumstances, but it was not simply His willingness to do God's will. It was His desire to serve His Father that motivated Him.

Jesus uses the Aramaic word "Abba," which is a term of deep affection and intimacy—much like our word "Daddy."[25] Jesus is saying, "Daddy, this is really hard! I need your help!" It was more than an act of His will—it was an expression of His love! It was the depth of His relationship with His father that inspired Jesus. This gave Him the power to go on, and granted Him the grace to meet intense suffering and profound injustice with strength and mercy.

Love was the motivator. Love was the driving force. And we're not talking about some abstract universal love. What we see in the garden is a deeply personal, intimate, connected love between the Father and the Son, between a daddy and his beloved child. This is so important: When Jesus teaches His followers to pray, He starts with "our Father." Not "my Father" or "the Father"—our Father. God is not only the Father of all humankind. He is Jesus's own Dad, and yours, and mine. He is truly our Father.

---

25 Kim and I were in Israel on a tour recently. While we are on the banks of the Jordan river, we heard a young Jewish boy shouting, "Abba, Abba, Abba!" as he ran after his Father. It was a precious reminder of the passion and intimacy of this word.

What's so amazing is that this is the kind of relationship God our Heavenly Father wants to have with us too! We begin by letting God love us—by choosing to believe His love for us is true.

The Apostle Paul says it this way: "The mature children of God are those who are moved by the impulses of the Holy Spirit. And you did not receive the 'spirit of religious duty,' leading you back into the fear of never being good enough. But you have received the 'Spirit of full acceptance,' enfolding you into the family of God. And you will never feel orphaned, for as he rises up within us, our spirits join him in saying the words of tender affection, 'Beloved Father!' For the Holy Spirit makes God's fatherhood real to us as he whispers into our innermost being, 'You are God's beloved child!'"[26]

Unfortunately for many of us, the idea of being a beloved child in relationship with a loving father is difficult to grasp. Our perspective of God as Father is greatly influenced early on by our relationship with our earthly fathers.

If your father was absent, you may view God as distant, impersonal and irrelevant. When things don't go your way, you might even have anger at God for His apparent lack of care. If your father was angry, you may want to avoid God, keeping a "safe distance" in your relationship. Fathers who parent with a high standard of performance and award or withhold their affections accordingly give us a distorted image of a God. We might think God approves of us only when we are "good" or high-achieving and is angry with us when we fail. Even doting fathers who are loving, accepting, and present can cause us shock and frustration when God allows us to go through difficult times. We think, "If God really loved me, He wouldn't let me experience this pain!"

Whether you were blessed by having a great dad, or were deprived of the loving presence you needed, your view of God as Father was shaped by your life experiences. So learning to live in the Kingdom of God, in submission to God the Father, means moving beyond your earthly parents and understanding who He really is—and who He really wants to be for you.

A few years ago, my father suddenly passed away at the young age of sixty-five. His loss was difficult to process. Standing 6'2" tall and 250 pounds, he had always been a pillar of security and stability. He was very present physically, and he and mom were inseparable. His "love language" was touch—he expressed his love and affection for me and my siblings with hugs or pats on the shoulder. He volunteered to serve in the U.S. Army at a time when many were doing what they could to avoid the draft. He was a defender of the downtrodden and a true servant.

Like the rest of us, he had his flaws. For reasons none of us can understand, deep inside he never felt accepted, never felt he belonged. Though he never spoke it, it was as if he felt he was fighting "the man" who was holding him down. I suspect this was something that developed out of his relationship with his father. Whatever the source, he wore this self-imposed rejection like some badge of honor.

When I was a senior in high school, the business he owned failed. Neither I nor any of my siblings were aware the business was in crisis. But literally overnight we went from a successful, middle-class lifestyle into barely surviving. We lost our cars, our home, everything. The chip he carried on his shoulder became a boulder crushing his spirit. He responded by seeking to protect the hurting and blaming "the man." Unfortunately for our relationship, it seemed I fell into the latter category.

Looking back, especially now that I have the perspective that comes from being a parent and provider, I can see how the stress of running a struggling family business caused my dad to withdraw emotionally. But at the time, all I saw was a distant, angry man who spoke of love but demonstrated emotional absence and a sharply critical nature. This—coupled with my first-born, strong-willed, driven personality—created a perfect storm of conflict during my formative teenage years.

Dad often expressed affection, but never pride or acceptance. In fact, the more successful I became the more he offered his corrective "balance" to keep me humble. My spiritual journey, marriage, career, and parenting efforts were all regular targets for his critique. I desperately wanted his approval, and that need drove me to prove that I was worthy of it.

I emerged with a view of God the Distant Provider. His love was expressed in His provision, but He was quite busy running the universe. His wrath was to be avoided at all costs. I was important to Him only in the sense that I was one of billions of other humans. If God was going to notice me personally, I was going to have to do something spectacular to get on His radar. Above all else, I believed, never fail! Failure meant getting His attention for all the wrong reasons.

While you may or may not be able to relate to my experiences, you certainly have your own! Maybe you were emotionally neglected or physically abandoned and continue to feel like an orphan, always waiting for the other shoe to drop: "Sure, things are okay now, but you never know when the rug is going to get pulled out from under you."

Maybe you felt ignored, rejected, or constantly judged against the successes of others. Statements like, "I wish you were more like your brother" imply that we are always less than acceptable. Maybe you were abused and rigorously controlled. As a pastor, I've seen these people respond by shutting down emotionally and by totally rebelling.

Maybe you are among those who have been fortunate enough to have a close, loving relationship with your dad. This is a wonderful blessing, but we all have to recognize that our parents were not perfect. There are aspects of our view of God that will take real work to reshape.

For better or worse—and usually both—your experiences with your father formed your view of God, our Heavenly Father. And all too often, your experiences distort your perception of God. Ask yourself: What expectations, assumptions, and filters have you created between you and God that might need to change? The process begins by first acknowledging that our view of God as Father is likely to be skewed or incomplete. Then we choose to believe God is a good Father, and we open ourselves up to becoming His children.

God fully accepts you. Through Christ you have been granted free access into His presence, but He really wants to be your Heavenly Father, your Dad, your Papa. He wants to love, guide, and provide for you, His beloved child. This shift in perspective transforms our relationship with God: we go from viewing Him as a benevolent deity we turn to when all else fails, to an intimate connection where we invite Him into every decision, discussion, relationship, and opportunity—every day. We turn to Him first because we know He cares. We embrace His guidance and direction because we know He has our back (and front and every side).

He counts the number of hairs on your head. Psalm 139:13 reminds us that God "formed my innermost being, shaping my delicate inside and my intricate outside, and wove them all together in my mother's womb." He was there at the moment of your conception, weaving your DNA together, creating a perfectly wonderful you. He crafted your personality, gave you unique talents, and walks with you through every challenge. He promises to turn all adversity you face into good: "We know that in all things God works for the good of those who love him, who have been called according to his purpose."[27]

He is aware of your every thought, feeling, and movement. He tells us that "not even one sparrow falls from its nest without the knowledge of your Father. Aren't you worth much more to God than many sparrows? So don't worry. For your Father cares deeply about even the smallest detail of your life."[28]

In Ephesians 2:10, He calls you His "poetry." He is dedicated to providing for you, caring for you, growing you, and leading you into a life of purpose, blessing, and fulfillment! Our God is an awesome God. Our Dad is an incredible Dad. Once we can see God for who He really is—and who He really wants to be for us—how can we do anything other than run to Him and live in the protection and provision of His Kingdom?

27 Romans 8:28
28 Matthew 10:29-31

CHAPTER FOUR

Living in the Kingdom

"What wealth is offered to you when you feel your spiritual poverty!
For there is no charge to enter the realm of heaven's kingdom. What
delight comes to you when you wait upon the Lord! For you will find
what you long for."
~ Matthew 5:3-4

I love the way Jesus talks: He likes to make us think! "What wealth [what blessing] is offered to you when you feel your spiritual poverty!" This is the opening line to His famous "Sermon on the Mount" found in Matthew chapter 5, and it encapsulates perfectly the lessons He is about to offer us.

If you've ever given a speech or put together an important presentation for work or school, you know that the first line is critical. It should sum up your topic, capture your audience's attention, and set up the framework for your thesis.

Jesus is laying out God's entire plan for mankind in this wondrous sermon, and he starts by offering what? Wealth! Now, when we see the word wealth we may want to automatically equate it with money. But that's not what Jesus is focusing on. Digging deeper, we see that the Greek word for "wealth" means "to be blessed, privileged, fortunate and happy regardless of one's circumstances." It is a translation from Aramaic word *toowayhon*,[29] which implies "great happiness, prosperity, abundant goodness, and delight." The word bliss captures all of this meaning. *Toowayhon*

---

29 The New Testament was written in Greek, the language of the day. However, Jesus would have preached in his native Aramaic language to the crowd. We often see this in the New Testament.

means to have the capacity to enjoy union and communion with God.[30]

So, here's Jesus' point: God is offering us the opportunity to live in bliss, to be blessed, to be wealthy with the abundant goodness of life. How do we find this wonderful perfection? It's simple, really: we have to be open to receiving it. And to do that, we need to recognize our own "spiritual poverty." Acknowledging our total inadequacy and our complete dependence upon God grants us access into the Kingdom of God and to His blessing. When we can recognize the reality of the magnitude of our own need, then we can enter into the place of God's provision. The opposite is also true. Not recognizing our need hides the entrance to the Kingdom of God.[31]

Jesus is intentionally setting up a stark contrast here between temporal wealth and spiritual poverty. He is saying when you recognize you truly have nothing and choose to depend upon God for everything, you receive more than you could ever imagine! The opposite is equally true. When you think you have it all together (or more commonly, when you think you have to have it all together to be accepted), you wind up with nothing.

None of us—not one—has what it takes on our own. But God has everything we could ever need and desire. Embracing that truth enables Him to bless us way beyond what we'd ever think to ask for or even imagine!

His next statement is equally powerful: "For there is no charge to enter the realm of heaven's kingdom." The Kingdom of God stands wide open. There is no charge to enter, no price we must pay to gain entry. It is perfectly free—because the admission fee was covered by Jesus Himself. All we have to do to enter God's Kingdom

---

30 Matthew 5:3, note a

31 Remember, not entering the Kingdom of God is not the same thing as not getting into Heaven when we die. We can be eternally saved and still live outside the Kingdom of God here on earth.

is recognize our lack, our need, and our inadequacy and accept His invitation. All we have to do is choose to depend upon the King for everything.

If you think back to Chapter 1, you'll notice that once again, there's nothing random about Jesus's choice of words. The Kingdom of God is a place. Not merely a state of mind or some distant, spiritual reality, but a finite location. It's the place we call Heaven, which transcends our physical world. It's the eternal destination of all those who have accepted Jesus as their Savior, and it is also available to us right here and now. It exists in our hearts, and through us, it extends to the world around us. The simplest way to sum up the Sermon on the Mount is: You will find blessing in the Kingdom of God, and you can enter that Kingdom right now.

Remember how tempting it is to think that these two worlds—our earthly life and our eternal life—are completely separate? It's easy to believe that Heaven is some distant, life-after-death concern which is completely irrelevant to our "real" life.

But we know this is all wrong. Looking at life this way is like seeing ourselves in a funhouse mirror. We may recognize aspects of our true selves, but the image is distorted. When we think of Heaven as a metaphysical place instead of a present reality, we completely misconstrue what God is up to in our lives.

Jesus tells us the Kingdom of God is something we can experience right now, without achieving perfection and without having to earn our right of entry. This cuts against the grain of our modern world, which is essentially a merit system: what we get out of life depends on what we put into it. We have to answer more than 90 percent of the questions correctly to ace the test. We have hit certain milestones before we can get a job, or a promotion, or a raise. Our value is measured by our contribution to the whole. Our success is evaluated by our ability to deliver more value than others do.

But that's not how God works! Certainly, he desires His children to be diligent, work hard, and serve others, but He's not sitting up there on His throne with a heavenly calculator, adding and subtracting points by the minute. He's an all-loving and all-merciful Father. He's not out to punish us for our failures and inadequacies, but to bless us because of His great love for us.

This realty came sharply into focus for me as a junior in high school. A teammate, who was an ultra-conservative pastor's son, had invited me and some of my closest friends to a Bible study at his home. After the snacks—a requirement for a group of always-hungry teenage boys—we sat down for our "study time." Our teammate, whom I believe truly meant well, began to list the sins we had all recently committed, emphasizing the impending reality of Hell that was soon to consume us all. If we were going to get on God's good side and experience His favor, he surmised, we had better change our ways and start living differently. Otherwise, God was going to reject us and there was no chance of entering Heaven.

The more he talked, the madder I became. I had no concept of theology, and I rarely read my Bible. Yet I knew deep down he was wrong! Wrong about God. Wrong about my friends. Wrong to spring his trap on us all. I blew a gasket! Shaking with anger, tears running down my cheeks, I railed against his view of God's Word. This was not the God I knew! God is not a lister of rules and punisher of failure. He is not a cold-hearted brute who exacts vengeance. He is not some eternal umpire making sure everyone follows the rules of His game, blowing the whistle on wrongdoers, putting them in His eternal penalty box.

God knew we were inadequate. He knew all our failures. It is why He sent Jesus, and it's why Jesus gave up His life on the cross. He says this in Luke 5:32: "I have not come to call the 'righteous,' but to call those who fail to measure up and bring them to repentance." Jesus knew we were a hot mess and took full responsibility for our sins! When we accept Him and receive His forgiveness for those sins, then we are back into relationship with God.

Needless to say, that was our last Bible study together, and it marked a significant shift in my pursuit of God. I knew He wanted me to do what was right and to not to sin—but this particular characterization of God's motivation bothered me tremendously.

He is a loving, kind, compassionate Father. He is a comforter and caregiver. Sure, He wants us to do what is right, but he doesn't hate us when we do wrong. He wants us to follow His commands so that we might walk in the full blessing of His provision. His commands and boundaries are for our benefit, not to limit our fun! God's laws don't restrict our freedom—they expand it. Psalm 119:45 sums it up beautifully, "I will walk with you in complete freedom, for I seek to follow your every command."

How do we know the Kingdom of God works this way? Because Jesus told us so! Let's look further at the Sermon on the Mount. He sat down on a hillside with His disciples gathered around Him, and crowds listening in, and showed us the benefits of living in the Kingdom of God during our earthly life. Let's listen in, too:

- *God blesses those who are poor and realize their need for him, for the Kingdom of Heaven is theirs.*
- *God blesses those who mourn, for they will be comforted.*
- *God blesses those who are humble, for they will inherit the whole earth.*

- *God blesses those who hunger and thirst for justice, for they will be satisfied.*
- *God blesses those who are merciful, for they will be shown mercy.*
- *God blesses those whose hearts are pure, for they will see God.*
- *God blesses those who work for peace, for they will be called the children of God.*
- *God blesses those who are persecuted for doing right, for the Kingdom of Heaven is theirs.*
- *God blesses you when people mock you and persecute you and lie about you and say all sorts of evil things against you because you are my followers. Be happy about it! Be very glad! For a great reward awaits you in heaven. And remember, the ancient prophets were persecuted in the same way.*[32]

"God blesses…" Over and over Jesus counts the ways. I love the way the Passion Translation shares these statements of Jesus:

- *What wealth is offered to you when you feel your spiritual poverty! For there is no charge to enter the realm of heaven's kingdom.*
- *What delight comes to you when you wait upon the Lord! For you will find what you long for.*
- *What blessing comes to you when gentleness lives in you! For you will inherit the earth.*
- *How enriched you are when you crave righteousness! For you will be surrounded with fruitfulness.*
- *How satisfied you are when you demonstrate tender mercy! For tender mercy will be demonstrated to you.*
- *What bliss you experience when your heart is pure! For then your eyes will open to see more and more of God.*

- *How blessed you are when you make peace! For then you will be recognized as a true child of God.*
- *How enriched you are when you bear the wounds of being persecuted for doing what is right! For that is when you experience the realm of heaven's kingdom.*
- *How ecstatic you can be when people insult and persecute you and speak all kinds of cruel lies about you because of your love for me! So leap for joy—since your heavenly reward is great. For you are being rejected the same way the prophets were before you.*

Look at these promises for those who choose to live in the Kingdom of God. You can live blessed, delighted, enriched, satisfied, ecstatic, leaping for joy! But what's just as important is what is not stated.

Jesus doesn't say, "You might be blessed someday." He doesn't say, "If you do these things, at some point in the future, maybe, you'll get into Heaven." No—this is a roadmap for living in blessing in the present and being assured of His promises in the future. If we do what He is teaching us to do, we get the benefit of experiencing His blessing now.

Jesus starts and ends with the present tense. "Blessed are the poor in spirit," Jesus announces, "for theirs is the kingdom of heaven." And he concludes with, "Blessed are those who are persecuted because of righteousness, for theirs is the kingdom of heaven."

In between, He lays out some of the challenges all human beings face at one point or another: poverty, mourning, persecution. And He assures us that when we place ourselves in God's presence, day by day—when we strive to be gentle, peaceable, merciful—God's blessings will surround us and sustain us. The Kingdom of God brings us comfort, satisfaction, and mercy. It draws us ever closer to God Himself.

Look at John 3:16-17: "For this is how much God loved the world—he gave his one and only, unique Son as a gift. So now everyone who believes in him will never perish but experience everlasting life. God did not send his Son into the world to judge and condemn the world, but to be its Savior and rescue it!" Jesus tells us once again that He isn't here to love those who are already perfect. And he assures us that God loves people so much, He wants them to "have" eternal life—to possess something in the *present tense*.

If we define "eternal life" as "the place where we go when we die," we completely miss the point. I have a car. I have a computer. I have a job. I have a family. And I have eternal life—right here, right now. Once we understand that Jesus is talking about having a rich, satisfying life right now, how does that change how we look at our life? It totally reframes it.

- *If I obey Jesus, I don't have to wait until I die: I can receive eternal blessings right here, right now.*
- *I already live in the Kingdom of Heaven: I can live in Heaven now because Jesus paid the price for me to be here.*
- *God is my Father, and I try my best to please Him because we love each other: when I fail, I express my regret and ask Him to help me grow.*
- *God and I live in the same place, and He cares about every detail of my life: my relationships, my job, my hobbies, my finances... everything!*
- *There is no separation between temporal life and my spiritual life: everything is unified in the Kingdom of Heaven.*

This is counterintuitive, and it's countercultural, too. Here's the bottom line: when we accept Jesus, we become citizens of Heaven. Our eternal destination is confirmed. We will live in God's universal Kingdom when we pass from this life...and we also have a passport to His particular Kingdom here and now!

It is our birthright, but it is also our choice. Just like Adam and Eve, we have free will. We can choose the Tree of Life or the Tree of the Knowledge of Good and Evil. Choosing Him seals our eternal destination. Yet how we choose to live each day determines whether we experience our present condition more like Heaven or more like Hell.

For some reason, we often make things harder than they have to be. We live in an age where no one likes to read the instructions. We expect everything to be intuitive and self-explanatory. But we ignore the manual at our own peril.

I recently purchased a new truck.[33] One of the features I was excited about was its remote start capability. Up in Amarillo, where we live, it gets quite cold in winter and hot in the summer. (Yes, there's snow in Texas!) Being able to let the car warm up or cool down before we get into it is a big deal. Try as I might, I could not find the right combination of buttons to activate the remote start. After twenty minutes of stubborn trial and error, I broke down and Googled it. Less than a minute later the car was warming up. By finally both learning and following the manufacturer's instructions, I activated a great feature on my new vehicle. The same is true of our lives.

God is our creator, and the Bible is our manual. It tells us everything we need to know to live in the fullness of blessing found in the center of His kingdom. The Kingdom of God is open to all who

---

33 If you must know, I got a Chevrolet Colorado ZR2, blacked-out edition. It is a very cool car.

accept Jesus. The first step is recognizing our spiritual poverty. Next comes learning and following His ways—not ours. When we learn God's ways and act on them, we activate the blessings he has for us right now.

Remember, "There is no charge to enter the realm of heaven's kingdom." So, when we choose Jesus, we begin our life in the Kingdom of Heaven. When we choose to learn His ways and obey His will, we receive the blessings he offers. Heaven awaits us, and Heaven is here in our midst.

All we need to do is say "yes."

CHAPTER FIVE

Growing in the Kingdom

So we are convinced that every detail of our lives is continually woven together to fit into God's perfect plan of bringing good into our lives, for we are his lovers who have been called to fulfill his designed purpose.

~ Romans 8:28

Living in the Kingdom of God means living in His blessing, but that does not mean that everything will be easy! Let's begin with a few truths.

First, God is good. His nature is good. His desires for you are good. His plan for you is good. Everything about Him is the very definition of goodness.

Second, he cares deeply, passionately, and intentionally about you, and about you fulfilling the purpose for which he created you. He's literally obsessed with you![34] Unlike us, God operates outside of time. He knows what you need in your future. He knows what gifts, talents, abilities, and opportunities you need. And He's a perfect coach who knows the exact exercise you need to perfect those things in you.

Third, He is the King, and we are not. Part of maturing is recognizing that it takes discipline to be successful. There is abundant grace, blessing, and help in God's Kingdom, but there is also a spiritual gym: a place where God puts us through the paces that

---

34 Obviously, God being "obsessed" is very different from us being obsessed. For us it means being solely focused on a specific person or thing to the exclusion of all other thoughts. God, because he is God, is able to focus perfectly on everyone at the same time. There is never a moment you are not on His mind and in His heart!

strengthen and prepare us for our future. Hebrews chapter 12 says, "Now all discipline [correction, instruction, training] seems to be more pain than pleasure at the time, yet later it will produce a transformation of character, bringing a harvest of righteousness and peace to those who yield to it."

A common misconception of our relationship with God is thinking that living in His blessing means never experiencing trials, struggles, and difficulties in life. This thinking leads us to believe that when life is good, God is blessing us, and when it's hard, He has turned away from us—or we have somehow failed Him and are being penalized. We approach God as if He is some genie in a bottle that we uncork when life gets difficult. We expect Him to pop out and fix it.

But the truth is He is always with us. It is during the many challenges of life that we get to lean on His strength and press into what he is trying to develop in us—even when it hurts.

Now, I am not talking about life's tragedies. We'll discuss that topic more in Chapter 9. I'm talking about the regular, day-to-day challenges we all face: a difficult boss, financial stress, relationship woes, physical limitations, bullying, flat tire or fender-bender, frustrating work assignment, or failed investment. These challenges can be occasional, sometimes seasonal, and every now and again completely overwhelming, as they seem to come at us like water from a fire hose.

We can view these challenges as problems or opportunities. We can, and should, ask God to deliver us from the struggles. But we should add to our prayer, "But not what I want. Let it be as you want, and if you want me to walk through this because you are teaching me something, Father, help me to learn quickly!" And we should remember that solutions and changes are often much slower to come than we wish.

The human body is an extraordinary thing. As I approached my forty-ninth birthday, I had a revelation. If I was going to accomplish the things God was calling me to, I was going to have to start paying a lot more attention to my physical self. My sedentary lifestyle, coupled with the normal entropy of aging, was compounding fast! My "big" clothes were getting snug. My blood pressure was ticking up. The doctor had me watching my cholesterol levels. I needed a serious shift. So, Kim and I joined a gym and found ourselves a trainer to show us what to do.

He immediately put us through various exercise routines: pushing, pulling, jumping, squatting, lifting, rowing. For an hour a day, three days a week, we were there sweating and straining—and it hurt! Every prescribed exercise pushed us to our physical limit, but that was not the hardest part. It was the soreness the next day! The simple act of standing up or walking across the room seemed torturous. Over time, as we progressed, the trainer made sure each exercise was more challenging than before, always pushing us to the next level.

I'm fascinated by the human body's amazing ability to repair itself. When our muscle fibers are placed under stress, the proteins are literally torn. The body recognizes this and begins to repair them, making them a bit stronger than before. Repeating this process of stress, damage, and healing over and over is what exercise is all about. We are a couple of years into this process now, and we're making a lot of progress!

I share this physical example because a similar reality exists in the Kingdom of God for our spiritual selves. God's the good Father who wants only what is best for us. Yet what's best is rarely the same as what's easiest. Now, He does not cause bad things to happen, but He knows that in a fallen world filled with fallen people who have the gift of free will, we will each have countless choices to make. We'll have countless opportunities to face challenges and press through to overcome them. When we lean into Him through these occasions, He teaches us, molds us, and graces us with the strength we need to overcome and endure what's happening. At the same time, he strengthens and equips us to handle even more the next round. Like a wonderful, divine coach, he guides us through life's exercises as he leads us toward maturity.

Understanding and embracing this maturing process is key to becoming spiritually and emotionally healthy. Rather than becoming angry or frustrated with God when we experience life's difficulties, we can learn to reach out for Him, listen for His voice, and absorb the lessons of the moment.

Consider the life of Joseph, beginning in Genesis 30. Born into privilege, he was Jacob's eleventh (and favorite) son, the eldest from his second wife Rachel. Generally speaking, picking a favorite out of twelve sons is not good parenting! It created tremendous tension between Joseph and his brothers. When he was seventeen, Joseph had a series of dreams in which he saw his father and older brothers bowing down to him. With the wisdom and humility of a spoiled teenager, he shared these dreams with his family. They were definitely not impressed.

To make things harder, Jacob gifted Joseph with a beautiful and expensive robe. This "coat of many colors" added insult to injury. His older brothers had had enough, and they began plotting to kill him.

One day, as Joseph came to meet his brothers out in the fields, they pounced! Stripping him of his fancy clothes, they threw him into a deep pit. They planned on letting him starve to death, but that day a caravan headed south to Egypt came through. Rather than kill Joseph and cover for their crime, they sold him to slave traders who hauled him off to Egypt and sold him to Potiphar, the captain of the guard for Pharaoh, king of Egypt. Within the space of twenty-four hours Joseph went from favored son to nameless slave in a foreign land. How unfair! How wrong! We can imagine him asking God, "Where are you? Why would you let this happen to me?"

Joseph had a choice to make. He could give up, complain, and grudgingly perform the minimal acts of servitude forced upon him. Or he could accept his circumstances and strive to do his best with the cards dealt him. To his credit, he chose to work diligently and apply all his energy to his position. God did not abandon him!

The Lord was with Joseph, so he succeeded in everything he did as he served in the home of his Egyptian master. Potiphar noticed this and realized that the Lord was with Joseph, giving him success in everything he did.

This pleased Potiphar, so he soon made Joseph his personal attendant. He put him in charge of his entire household and everything he owned. From the day Joseph was put in charge of his master's household and property, the Lord began to bless Potiphar's household for Joseph's sake. All his household affairs ran smoothly, and his crops and livestock flourished.

So Potiphar gave Joseph complete administrative responsibility over everything he owned. With Joseph there, he didn't worry about a thing—except what kind of food to eat![35]

---

35 Genesis 39:2-6 (NLT)

So, Joseph evolves into an up-and-comer blessed by the Lord and favored by the captain of the guard of Pharaoh himself. Things are looking up! At least they were…right up until Potiphar's wife tries to force him to have sex with her. She falsely accuses Joseph of impropriety and has him thrown into the king's personal prison. Once again, he is betrayed. Once again, he is tossed alone into the pit with no chance of a trial and no real hope of anyone even remembering he exists.

And once again, Joseph has a choice. Get angry with God and turn his back on Him? Or embrace his circumstances and rise to whatever occasion is available to him? Again, Joseph chooses right. He pours all his talent and energy into serving in the prison. And again, God blesses him:

But the Lord was with Joseph in the prison and showed him his faithful love. And the Lord made Joseph a favorite with the prison warden. Before long, the warden put Joseph in charge of all the other prisoners and over everything that happened in the prison. The warden had no more worries, because Joseph took care of everything. The Lord was with him and caused everything he did to succeed.[36]

Years later (not weeks or months!), Joseph has an opportunity to stand before Pharaoh and interpret a troubling dream the king had. He is hauled up out of prison and placed before the king. Joseph hears the dream, and God gives him the interpretation: Egypt and the surrounding lands are going to experience seven years of great prosperity followed by seven years of severe famine. Then Joseph lays out a fantastic plan for Pharaoh to capitalize on this opportunity, saving Egypt and greatly increasing Pharaoh's wealth and regional influence. Pharaoh and his court were blown away by Joseph's presentation. Here's how it played out:

> *Joseph's suggestions were well received by Pharaoh and his officials. So Pharaoh asked his officials, 'Can we find anyone else like this man so obviously filled with the spirit of God?'*
>
> *Then Pharaoh said to Joseph, 'Since God has revealed the meaning of the dreams to you, clearly no one else is as intelligent or wise as you are. You will be in charge of my court, and all my people will take orders from you. Only I, sitting on my throne, will have a rank higher than yours.' Pharaoh said to Joseph, 'I hereby put you in charge of the entire land of Egypt.'*
>
> *Then Pharaoh removed his signet ring from his hand and placed it on Joseph's finger. He dressed him in fine[37] linen clothing and hung a gold chain around his neck. Then he had Joseph ride in the chariot reserved for his second-in-command. And wherever Joseph went, the command was shouted, 'Kneel down!' So Pharaoh put Joseph in charge of all Egypt.*
>
> *And Pharaoh said to him, 'I am Pharaoh, but no one will lift a hand or foot in the entire land of Egypt without your approval.'*

Wow! Joseph just made it to the top of the big leagues! In one day, he went from being a desperate and despised prisoner to being the second highest in command of the most powerful country in the world.

---

37 Genesis 41:37-44 (NLT)

So, here's the question we have to ask ourselves: Which event was the blessing of God? Was it the betrayal of his brothers? Was it being sold into slavery? Was it the false accusations of his master's wife? Being forgotten in prison? Or was it the sudden promotion by Pharaoh? It is easy to see his promotion as God's blessing, but we have to look at the whole journey. God needed to prepare Joseph for his promotion. That means that every other action and circumstance—no matter how terrible or unjust—were used by God to shape, train, develop, and mature Joseph. Without the former challenges the latter blessing is simply not possible. Joseph would not have been ready to rise to the occasion.

In slavery, Joseph became the personal servant to Pharaoh's captain of the guard. It was there that he learned the precision of military discipline with its systems and structures. It was there that he developed a clear understanding of the role of chain-of-command. In the king's prison, he rubbed shoulders with numerous members of the king's court. He had an opportunity to hone his leadership skills and develop his personal leadership style. Most important, he learned the power of humility.

To stand before Pharaoh and presume to instruct him on the best course of action is absurd! So when we hear Joseph sharing his plan with Pharaoh, we can sense the deep humility of one who has endured much difficulty but chooses to trust in God in all things. He is no longer acting superior and presumptuous. He is simply offering God's interpretation of the dream—not looking for glory or taking credit for himself—and humbly suggesting a solution.

Joseph demonstrated two characteristics that qualified him for promotion. First, he was diligent in every life circumstance. It did not matter to him if it was "fair" or if the difficulty of his circumstances was his fault. Now, I am certain that like all of us, he struggled along the way, but he always chose to fully invest himself in the tasks at hand. Second, Joseph always trusted in God. He never wavered. He never second-guessed the Lord. He held steadfast to his faith in God's provision for him.

And in turn, God the Father—the great coach of mankind—used the difficult events of Joseph's life to shape him into the great leader that would rescue the entire Hebrew population. Joseph needed to experience adversity before he could embrace humility, and he needed to be humbled before he could be exalted.

The year 2006 was one of the most difficult in my life. It was one of those firehose years where everything seemed to be coming at us at once. Kim and I felt abandoned, rejected, and punished for doing what we believed to be right. We felt like we had heard God and obeyed Him, but we were rewarded with pain. Frankly, by May of that year, I was so angry with God that I quit praying. By August, I finally "forgave" God and began pursuing Him again, but it would be more than a year before we were vindicated and life began to resume something approaching normal.[38] It was awful.

Yet today, I can look back and clearly see how the thread that started in the most difficult of circumstances in 2006 led me directly to where I am today. I am doing what I love with people I love because of what happened years ago. If Joseph had skipped or shortened his time in slavery or prison, the parts of him that were critical for the salvation of Israel wouldn't have been fully formed. If I were to remove the difficulties of that year from my life, I would cease to be who I am. It's the pain that prepares us for the next role God has for us.

---

38 The very idea of "forgiving" God is bad theology. Clearly God does not do wrong and therefore has no need to be forgiven. Yet, I found that He is big enough to recognize that we are offended with Him, and thus, "forgiving" Him means putting *our* heart right. We "let" God off the hook for our pain, drop our anger, and accept His goodness in our lives, even if we are doing it by faith and not by sight.

In the Kingdom of God, only the King has the full perspective. Only He knows the story from beginning to end. Living in the Kingdom of God means submitting to the King as your teacher and trainer, someone who knows what's good for us more than we ourselves could know or understand. It means choosing to give it your all because you serve the King, even when your circumstances seem unfair or overwhelmingly hard. It means trusting God to shape and refine you during difficult times. It means giving up on your own desires for glory and self-promotion and fully depending on Him. Jesus says it to His disciples this way:

If you truly want to follow me, you should at once completely disown your own life. And you must be willing to share my cross and experience it as your own, as you continually surrender to my ways. For if you let your life go for my sake and for the sake of the gospel, you will continually experience true life. But if you choose to keep your life for yourself, you will forfeit what you try to keep. For what use is it to gain all the wealth and power of this world, with everything it could offer you, at the cost of your own life?[39]

Sharing His cross means choosing to die to the pursuit of our own glory and choosing to surrender the path of our life to Him. When we die to ourselves, we are ready to be raised up by the King.

The Kingdom of God is not a place of retreat but rather a place of growth and development. We won't find our calling and purpose down the easy road, but up the steep hill of adversity, just as Jesus did. And like Jesus, if we approach our trials with total trust in God the Father as our guide, we will triumph.

CHAPTER SIX

Identity Crisis

And as Jesus rose up out of the water, the heavenly realm opened up
over him and he saw the Holy Spirit descend out of the heavens and
rest upon him in the form of a dove. Then suddenly the voice of the
Father shouted from the sky, saying, "This is the Son I love, and my
greatest delight is in him."
~ Matthew 3:16,17

The Kingdom of God is where we discover who we are and who we were created to be. Our identity was handcrafted by God. There are no accidents or errors with God. Finding our identity in Him—seeing ourselves as he sees us—sets us on the path He destined for each of us to take.

When Jesus was twelve years old, Mary and Joseph took Him to Jerusalem to celebrate the feast of Passover. Here, Tween Jesus decided it was time to start studying with the rabbis to prepare for His ministry. Clearly, His parents had shared with Him something of His miraculous birth, God's amazing provision, and His future destiny. And Jesus believed it. After a full day of traveling toward home, Mary and Joseph realized Jesus was not with anyone in their family caravan. They returned to Jerusalem and found Him studying with the rabbis.

I love picturing Jesus as a young lad full of confidence and self-assurance, ready to take on the world. In His human immaturity, He felt it was time to take things into His own hands. Yet even Jesus needed His parents to guide Him.

They return home together, and the Bible fast-forwards to when Jesus is thirty years old—the age of adulthood in the Jewish tradition. Jesus meets up with His cousin John, who baptizes Him in the Jordan river. Coming up out of the water, Jesus and John hear the Heavenly Father loudly proclaim, "This is the Son I love..."[40]

When we're young, we all fantasize about who we want to be when we grow up: a fireman, princess, doctor, soldier, or maybe president. Me, I wanted to be an architect. My dad was an electrical contractor and home builder. He had a drafting table in his office at our home. I'd go in and begin to draw, pretending I was designing some great structure.

There is a strong desire within each of our souls to know who we are and who we are meant to be. What will my contribution to society be? How will the world be different because I was a part of it? How will I be remembered? We desire to belong but also to stand out; to be a part of the whole and yet leave our individual, indelible mark on the world.

Just take a quick glance through your favorite social media platform. People are working so hard to broadcast their "brand" to the world. World adventurer traveling to exotic locales. Budding artist. Fitness guru. Daredevil. Super-parent. Fashionista. Culinary genius. There's even a word for it now: "influencer." We see so many people striving to be the most liked, the most influential, the most validated, the most desirable, the most valuable.

Every single one of us has a built-in desire to positively affect the world. It's part of God's hardwiring into the human psyche—it goes all the way back to creation. Genesis 1:28 says, "Then God blessed [mankind] and said, 'Be fruitful and multiply. Fill the earth and govern it. Reign over the fish in the sea, the birds in the sky, and all the animals that scurry along the ground.'" We were created to govern and reign. While it can turn to vanity, the root of the desire comes from the Creator Himself. The challenge is finding specifically what we were created to do—or more accurately, who we were created to be.

A lucky few of us come across their identity by chance, and seem to find great joy and fulfillment easily. Others spend a lifetime searching, trying on different identities for size only to end up frustrated, disillusioned, and cynical. Most of us find ourselves somewhere along the spectrum between those two extremes.

Jesus was no different. He knew he was unique—fully God and fully man, with a divine mission and purpose. He knew who His real father was. He knew He was the Son of God. He had heard the stories of the angels in the fields singing about His birth. He had seen the ornate crates that held the gifts of the Magi. He knew of His family's flight to Egypt to avoid King Herod's wrath. Entering adulthood, He had a miraculous confirmation from Heaven: "This is my Son." Could it be possible that His human side still wondered, still had some lingering doubts?

You might think that with all this miraculous confirmation, Jesus would be fully confident in His identity, that He would not be tempted to believe otherwise. But He did, and Satan saw it as an opportunity.

Immediately following Jesus' heavenly confirmation of His identity, the Holy Spirit leads Him into the desert wilderness to fast and pray for forty days. Along the way, Satan shows up to tempt Him. In Matthew 4, Satan specifically targets Jesus's faith by questioning His identity, challenging Him with three progressive propositions:

"How can you possibly be the Son of God and go hungry? Just order these stones to be turned into loaves of bread." (verse 3)

"If you're really God's Son, jump, and the angels will catch you. For it is written in the Scriptures: 'He will command his angels to protect you and they will lift you up so that you won't even bruise your foot on a rock.'" (verse 6)

"All of [kingdoms of the world] I will give to you," the accuser said, "if only you will kneel down before me and worship me." (verse 9)

Jesus had to battle against these temptations. Just as when Satan tempts us, he did not show up in a recognizable form. It's likely it seemed to Jesus to be His own voice whispering in some internal conversation. We can imagine Jesus, hungry from His fast, looking longing at a stone thinking, "If I really am the Son of God, I could command that rock to be bread and it would be so!" Jesus processes this possibility, then decides against the power demonstration by proclaiming, "Man does not live on bread alone!"

Next, Jesus heads to the Temple Mount in Jerusalem and finds Himself standing on the precipice of the wall several stories above the ground! There would have been hundreds of people milling around below. Suddenly this thought comes into His head: "You know, scripture says God's angels will protect the Son of God, keeping his foot from even being bruised on a rock. If I jump off this ledge—and if I am truly the Son of God—the angels would have to show up and save me. All these people below would see the show, and I would be recognized as someone awesome." The next thought corrects His thinking and He speaks: "Wait. No. Scripture also says, 'Don't put your God to the test.'"

Finally, Jesus is taken up into a vision and able to see all the kingdoms of the earth. He instantly knows that if He were to choose to worship Satan, He could lead the world without having to suffer and die for the sins of man. This time He recognizes Satan's scheming and speaks directly to him, "Go away, enemy! For the Scriptures say: Kneel before the Lord your God and worship only Him."[41]

Satan is crafty! Look at the form of Jesus's temptation: demonstrate what you can do to show the world who you are. I beg you not to rush past this! Jesus—the Son of God, Creator of the Universe, the Alpha and Omega, the Messiah—was wrestling with His identity at age thirty. Satan's plan was to trap Him into working to prove who He already was.

If the devil tried that trick on Jesus, don't you think he tries it on us as well? If Satan can get us working to prove who we are, he can get us to shift the source of our identity from God to our performance: in other words, to ourselves. The source of your identity is also the source of your power and authority. You must choose your source with deliberation and care.

I was conceived and born in Germany while my father was stationed at Ramstein Air Force base serving in the U.S. Army. As a teen, I read that I could choose to have dual citizenship in both countries if I wanted to. It seemed like a grand idea at the time. I could have two passports! I could travel across Europe as a European! Most important, it seemed really cool. Then I read the fine print. As a citizen, I had the rights, privileges, and responsibilities of citizenship. I would need to pay taxes, serve in their military as required, adhere to their laws. With dual citizenship, I would be beholden to two countries. It was more responsibility than I wanted.

Our identity comes from our citizenship. I am American because my parents were Americans, and I have a birth certificate

---

that proves it. My driver's license was granted by the State of Texas because that's my home. My passport comes from the United States of America. My identity—who I am—is a function of my heritage, coupled with the governing authorities determining my citizenship.

Let's backtrack a bit to Jesus and His temptation. Satan came to tempt the Son of God to use His power to validate His identity: to do something to prove who He was. Here's the problem with that: When we rely on our abilities to establish our identity, our power and authority are based on our performance, not our citizenship. This creates a false, pseudo-identity that is derived completely from much or how little we achieve. Making matters far worse, our identity then becomes subjective. Our performance is constantly being judged by an often hostile and ever-changing world. In this environment, finding our identity is like trying to see our reflection in fast-moving water. We catch glimpses every now and again, but mostly all we see is a blur.

The real victory for Jesus was believing in who He was without any demonstration of power. Now, we know Jesus performed hundreds, if not thousands, of miracles during His three years of ministry. It would have been easy for Him to get His validation through the powerful acts He performed and the admiration of the witnesses who saw His miracles. But He never did! He was anchored in the recognition of who He was regardless of what He did. He was God's beloved Son. Secure in his identity, He worked wonders to prove to us that He was who He said He was—not to prove it to Himself.

Many years ago, I woke up with these words pounding in my head: "Who, What, When, Where, How!" Now, I was used to hearing the Lord speak to me, but not like this. Not before coffee. He was interrupting my morning, and He had something He wanted me to hear. I settled in, got my journal, and said, "Okay, Father, whatcha got?"

He instantly responded, "Which is missing?"

I thought, "Who, what, when, where, how... why. *Why* is missing."

"Exactly!" He responded, "You don't get to ask my why. My ways are higher than your ways. My thoughts are higher than your thoughts. It's not that I don't want to tell you why or that I am purposefully withholding something from you. You are simply not equipped to comprehend the why. You just have to trust me."

"Great. I see that." But there was more the Lord wanted me to see.

"Now, look at the order of the others." He said, "First comes *who*. This is the most important question for you to ponder. This is what I want to talk about with you and reinforce in you. Who you really are. Who you really are in Me. Next comes *what* you do. *What* always follows *who*. Then come the *when* and *where*. These are together, but timing comes before location. Remember Abraham: he went to a land I would show him later. The going came before knowing the location."

God continued, "Finally, we have *how*. I'm not really a fan of discussing how, but I know you are weak and have doubts. So we can occasionally talk about how I'm going to do things in your life. Just know it will be a limited discussion. I would much rather talk about who you are to Me!"

God showed me through this experience the incredible power in receiving our "who" from Him. It is simultaneously empowering and freeing. It is empowering in that I know I am welcome and accepted in the Kingdom of God by the King Himself, and it's freeing because I can stop trying so hard to prove to others—and to myself—how important I really am. I'm very valuable to Him, and that is more than enough.

This conversation has had a profound impact on my life. He also showed me how in our earth-bound attempt to find our identity, we normally go through the exact opposite progression. We start with *why*. Why? Because I want to be happy. I want to be fulfilled. I want what's best for me. We even give bad advice to one another. "Do whatever makes you happy." We establish the *why*, and we set about trying different ways of how to achieve it. Today it's travel. Tomorrow it's sex. We try this group of friends, then that group. We go to school to get a degree and figure out a career. Surely that's the right *how* to find success, right?

Once we zoom in on our *how*, we look for the best *where*—the best place to experience it. We seek a specific school, career path, or city. Next we consider the timing—the when. "As soon as I get enough money, I'm going to move there, find the right home, and finally start my life," we say. All the while, our reason—our why—for seeking happiness and fulfillment drums mercilessly in our hearts.

We finally settle into our *what*. What we do. What makes us special. And without even realizing it, we find our life being defined by the things we do. Our activities and achievements establish our identity, and the painful irony is that we hardly recognize ourselves in the very life we have so purposefully crafted. By letting our achievements define us, we inadvertently lose who we really are somewhere along the path of our pursuit of happiness.

I spent the first five years of my marriage to Kim pouring myself into my career. I told her—and myself—that I was doing it for "us." But really, deep down, I hoped that if I could achieve success through money, personal fulfillment, and recognition by people I deemed important then I would finally be able to prove that I was valuable. This pursuit turned me into selfish near-narcissist. Only after nearly wrecking my marriage did I humble myself and turn to God to find my worth.

There is tremendous power and authority that comes from knowing who you are and what you are worth. So, who are you?

In the Kingdom of God, our identity is established by none other than the King Himself! Like Jesus, we must embrace our identity first and let our purpose be defined and established inside that reality. The reality that we are special for who we are, not what we do. That we are loved by God as His beloved creation, not His robotic workforce. Once we absorb that truth, we can move with the power and authority of a citizen of Heaven, secure in our identity. We can approach the what of our created purpose without the baggage of being beholden to the whims of those who judge us for it.

The instant you accept Jesus as your Lord and Savior, you become a citizen of the Kingdom of God. You are already a beloved child of the King. Your brother is the Son of God, and the Son of Man. You are a co-heir with Him. You are a favored member of the royal family. You're a member of the Royal Priesthood of Heaven. You are an ambassador for Christ, representing His heavenly interests here on the earth.

You are a masterful work of art handcrafted by the Creator of the universe Himself. You were created on purpose and for a purpose. You are loved, provided for, and fully accepted. You're special, unique, and wonderful. You are known. You are amazing.

It is so freeing to live as a citizen of Heaven. Embrace your heavenly passport! Receive your heavenly identity. It truly is the key to finding the joy that satisfies your soul, and the peace that surpasses all understanding.

CHAPTER SEVEN

Pursuing Your Purpose

Jesus answered him, "The most important of all the commandments is this: 'The Lord Yahweh, our God, is one!' 30 You are to love the Lord Yahweh, your God, with every passion of your heart, with all the energy of your being, with every thought that is within you, and with all your strength. This is the great and supreme commandment. 31 And the second is this: 'You must love your neighbor in the same way you love yourself.' You will never find a greater commandment than these."

~ Mark 12:29-31

We know by now that our identity is grounded in and guided by the King. That's who we are—but how do we know what we're supposed to do? What's our purpose? We all have an innate desire to make a difference in the world and for our lives to matter. And if we're honest, we want to be important, counted upon, recognized, remembered. This desire is hardwired into us by God Himself. It is a natural progression for us to move from accepting our identity to seeking out our God-given purpose.

Think back to the question that likely popped up throughout your childhood: What do you want to be when you grew up? A princess? A fireman? A doctor? A teacher? Coach? Military commander? Superman? No one had to teach us to pretend to be these people. Our playtime was not structured by rules or influenced by the need for a paycheck. We simply dreamed of a time when we could influence on the world around us, and we idolized people and professions that seemed to really matter.

We imagined a time when we would be free from the constraints of our parents and family life. No room to clean, chores to do, or homework to finish. We would spend our time teaching, helping, and saving people. We would be loved, appreciated, and rewarded for our service to others.

And then somewhere along the way—likely around middle to early high school—we were encouraged to stop dreaming and start focusing. College was just around the corner, and we needed to be ready.

The pressure on average teenagers to decide what they are going to be when they grow up is tremendous! We take tests designed to highlight our potential career matches. Have an aptitude for tactical work? You'd be a great mechanic. Have a nurturing temperament? Pursue nursing. Really good at math? You'd make a solid engineer.

Then—suddenly—you find yourself grown up. You're done with school, and working in your first (or maybe second) job. You might be a young couple with a child or two. You have bills and loans to pay and you're facing the stark reality that your resources of time, money, and experience are quite limited. Opportunities for advancement tend to come much more slowly than you anticipated. Yet all the pressure to "be somebody" and to "make a difference in the world" is still crushing down on you!

Compounding this negative cycle is our modern obsession with personal branding. In a single generation, social media has remapped our entire social framework. We all have control over the version of ourselves that we broadcast to the world. On the one hand, this is amazing! We can share our lives with friends and relatives across the globe. We can experience life and see the world through another's perspective. On the other hand, it focuses our attention not on God, but on ourselves. And how much of it is actually real?

A couple of years ago, my college-aged son went to the beach on the Texas Gulf Coast with his friends over a long weekend. Kim and I tracked the fun they were having through their social media posts. All the classic images were there—beach sunsets, gentle waves, friends playing catch on the sand. Everyone was clearly having a blast. After he returned to school, he texted us pictures of his legs and back. He had accumulated hundreds (if not thousands) of sand-flea bites! Apparently, he and his friends all had the same problem: what to do about all the itching! Beneath the projected nirvana of a beach getaway was the scratchy reality of a sand-flea infestation. No one wanted a picture of that!

Think about this. If you are in your twenties or early thirties, you face a challenge that the generations before you did not confront. Three forces are converging: First, you have a God-given desire to make a difference in the world. This is normal and right. Second, you faced tremendous pressure at a very young age to select your "perfect" life-path—an impossible task. It is likely that pressure is still present somewhere in the recesses of your psyche, creating negative self-judgment and bearing down upon your self-esteem. Third, you are surrounded by the carefully curated images of your friends and "influencers" who appear to have reached the pinnacle of life. It seems everyone but you has life all figured out. Wow! What a trap!

Here we come to the heart of the matter. How do we achieve success? And how do we measure it? To answer these important questions, we have to first define what success is. And this is the question of the ages: Aristotle and Plato believed that achieving personal happiness was the highest aim of humanity. Socrates took things a step further, believing that happiness comes not from merely satisfying our desires but from understanding how we think and feel about those desires. Buddhism's teachings on happiness go deeper into developing one's inner thought life, concluding that "pure" thoughts produce happiness.

Notice the similarity in both the western and eastern philosophies on success: they all frame "happiness" as the ultimate aim of human existence. We tend to boil all this into a simple catchphrase spoken as if it was true wisdom: "Do what makes you happy." That's really bad advice. How in the world am I ever going to find out what it is that makes me happy? And as all of us know, just because something makes us feel happy in the moment does make it objectively good, worthy, or right. Things that bring momentary pleasure are sometimes quite damaging to us (or to others).

Even the process of chasing happiness is deeply flawed. It suggests a lifetime of trial and error, of segmenting our lives into seasons of pursuit. Maybe sex will make me happy. Certainly, that's what the entertainment industry often suggests. How about money? Once I'm rich enough, my problems will diminish, my opportunities will increase, and then I will be happy all the time. Right?

We're told over and over how important it is to find the right, fulfilling career. The perfect job that feels more like a mission where all the work is enjoyable, productive, and encouraging. A place filled with satisfied, encouraging, and committed people. Surely, we tell ourselves, if I could just find the right gig, then happiness will find me!

Yet all of this amounts to chasing after an elusive dream: something that seems just around the corner, over the next hill, somewhere on the horizon. In reality, it's perfectly unattainable and permanently out of reach. By the time we come to realize that sex, travel, entertainment, status, and money don't produce the fulfillment we are seeking, we have wasted a good portion of our productive lives. This frustration can lead to depression, anxiety, escapism. So we turn to food, alcohol, drugs, gaming, endless social media spinning...we'll do whatever it takes to keep our mind off our perceived failure to find true happiness and success.

I'm getting stressed out just thinking about it. So let's hit pause. Take a deep breath and back up a few steps. Where did things go sideways? Think back to your childhood dreams of becoming a princess, police officer, coach, nurse, or doctor. Why did you want to be those things? You were likely not thinking about money, travel, or influence back then. Success was not measured by how important you were. No, it was measured by how much you could help others. Importance was measured not in influence but in service. To protect. To heal. To defend. To nurture. To entertain. To improve. To save. Those were our motivations.

The assumption that were are here to find happiness is so deeply woven into the framework of our western culture that it influences our definition of truth. The educators who encouraged you to take an aptitude test in the eighth grade were not intentionally trying to force you into some box. They believed they were giving you the best opportunity to find fulfillment later in life. But again, the system is built on the premise that happiness is the highest human goal and that doing what we are best at will produce it.

But what if finding happiness is not the highest goal? What if it was never meant to be our purpose? What if the pursuit of happiness is actually the exact opposite of what we are supposed to be about? Then the entire system comes crashing down.

The fatal flaw in the pursuit of happiness is that we find ourselves in the center of the activity. I focus on what makes me happy, or at least what I think will make me happy. I am both the focus and measure of success. But the Kingdom of God operates the opposite way. God is the King. He is the center. He defines success. Think back to our discussion on the Sermon on the Mount in Chapter 4: Each of these blessings and promises are based upon us putting God first and loving other people well. This is the basis of success in the Kingdom of God.

Let's go a little further: If we define success as "the accomplishment of an aim or purpose," then I'm the one who gets to measure it. I decide whether I've accomplished my goals. No rocket science here. We are meant to pursue our unique purpose—not our individual happiness.

I used to drive a fun two-door, six-speed sports car. We're talking a manual transmission, precision-crafted, German-engineered thing of beauty. I'd always dreamed of having something like it, something that went from zero to 60 mph in ... whatever. Faster than I ever really needed to get to 60 mph (or maybe a bit higher on the West Texas country roads).

One day on the way to the office, I ended up at a stoplight as the first car on the line. A friend of mine happened to pull up in the lane beside me in his big Ford F-150 King Ranch pickup truck. Feeling a little cocky, I quickly texted him, "Wanna race?"

His replied instantly: "Absolutely! But I get to pick the dirt road."

What a brilliant response! Clearly my car had his truck beat in a street race, but his truck would easily have had my car on a dirt road (three inches of clearance is not much). Success depended upon the purpose for which each automobile was designed.

Ask yourself: for what purpose were you designed? It is only when we understand our purpose that we can determine how we each should measure success.

Look back at the verse in Mark we used to begin this chapter. The religious leader had just asked Jesus which of the commandments were the greatest. You can almost hear him asking, "Jesus, what's the point? Can you sum this all up for me? Why are we here? What do I need to do to achieve success in life?"

The first half of Jesus's response was predictable. "The Lord our God is one. Love God with all your passion, energy, thoughts and strength." This was part of a common Jewish prayer called the *shema*. "Hear, O Israel: The Lord is our God, the Lord alone." It is spoken at the beginning of Jewish services and placed on the doorpost of their homes. The *shema* forms the foundation of Judaism. Every devout Jew would have agreed with Jesus. This is the most important thing for everyone to do. No arguments there.

But then, as usual, Jesus surprised the crowd by adding this: "Love your neighbor as you love yourself." This was shocking! No rabbi had ever combined these two concepts. Jesus was essentially saying, "The single most important thing in life is to love God with everything you've got and also love the people around you like you love yourself." The two commandments are inseparable.[42]

The religious leader was blown away by Jesus's statement. It made tremendous sense to him, and he told Jesus, "Teacher, how beautifully you have answered!" And how did Jesus react? By pointing him back to the Kingdom of God. "When Jesus noticed how thoughtfully and sincerely the man answered, he said to

---

42 For an interesting view of this, look up the Matthew version of the "Great Commandment" found in Matthew 22:34-40. Matthew, speaking of the second commandment, says it is "equally important." The Greek word used for equally important is *homoia*, from which we get our word *homogeneous*, which means inseparable.

him, 'You're not far from the reality of God's kingdom realm.'"
(Mark 12:34)

Ah, there it is! There's our answer. The Kingdom of God—God's kingdom realm—is where we can find our purpose. Each of us was lovingly designed and brought into existence by God for the purpose of loving Him back, with all our passion, energy, thoughts, and strength, and loving others as we love ourselves.

Life is not about how important we are, how much influence we have, or how free we are from the limitations of money, time, or experience. It's about how well we actively love and serve people! That is what Jesus was saying!

Our purpose is to love. We were created to love: to love God, others, ourselves. How much and how often and how deeply we love is the true measure of our success. The amazingly good news, then, is that what we "do" doesn't really matter—at least not in terms of how the world measures success. What matters is how we treat and serve the people we live our lives with. Our friends, family, and neighbors. The folks we encounter each day at our jobs, grocery stores, restaurants, and churches. It is the investments we make in other people that determine our success.

Now let's go one step further. If my purpose is to love, then I need to really understand what love is. If it is simply an emotion, an evaluation of how I feel about people, then we're right back where we started. The emotional experience of loving and being loved is simply redefining what we mean by happiness. So, loving in the Kingdom of God has to be something more than how we feel.

I recently heard a pastor ask a group this question, "What is the verb of the Bible?"

The immediate response from the crowd, myself included, was, "to love." We were close, but not quite right. He took us to John

3:16, one of the most famous verses in the Bible: "For this is how much God loved the world—he gave his one and only, unique Son as a gift." Love is God's motivation, but the verb—the action demonstrating it—is giving. True love, therefore, is giving of yourself to others for their benefit.

God gave us His only son for our benefit. He held nothing back. He gave His very best because He loved us without reservation. In the Kingdom of God, love always motivates us to give ourselves to others, solely for their benefit.

Understanding this changes everything. The skills I need to be successful are not the ones I learned in high school or college. Depending on the quality of your family life growing up, it's not a given that you learned much there either. If we measure our success by the depth of our love, then my interpersonal skills, like empathy, compassion, and active listening, are what are more important than anything else I could do or have.[43]

During the mid 1990s, the company where I worked as a mid-level manager got a new general manager. He had decades of big company experience and had recently sold his startup company. A West Point graduate and retired brigadier general in the Army, he had cut his business teeth selling cameras and supplies to the camera shops in Manhattan—a tough market to say the least! Intelligent, disciplined, and driven, he was just what the owner thought we needed.

He was also a colossal jerk! He cussed, yelled, slammed his fist on the table regularly, and berated employees publicly. No nonsense, no excuses, no grace.

---

43 It turns out modern business science agrees with this assessment. The whole concept of "emotional intelligence" is based upon it. A quick Google search will give you tons of information on this topic. Many of Patrick Lencioni's books also touch on this concept. Another great source is Simon Sinek.

After a few months, I'd had all I could take. I loved my job, but this was too much. I went into his office to present him with the results of a project I had been assigned. He didn't like the way I had done it. He started his usual yelling and cussing, and I snapped! I shouted back at him, "Hey, I'll do this project any way you want. I am happy to change it and glad to learn! I am glad to serve you any way I can, but I don't like being cussed at! Where I come from those are fighting words, and I'm here to help you and this company, not fight with you!"

I was sure he would fire me on the spot. He didn't. In fact, his attitude toward me changed in an instant, and he became one of the greatest mentors I ever had. To my recollection, he never raised his voice to me again.

Two years later, he and I traveled to New York City to investigate a potential acquisition. When he learned I had never been to the Big Apple, he scheduled us to get in day early so he could give me a personal tour. We walked around for hours—Central Park, Rockefeller Center, all the way down to the Empire State Building. On our way back to the hotel, he stopped on the sidewalk and said, "See that window up there on the corner of that building? The one on the third floor?"

"Yes, sir," I answered. And then he said something that left me speechless: "That used to be my wife's office. I would come and stand here looking up for her. She would wave, come down, and we'd go to lunch. I miss those days." We just stood there for several moments with me fighting back the tears. Even today, I still feel his deep pain.

I knew she had lost a battle with cancer about ten years earlier. He had quit his high-paying job as the vice president of sales for one of the world's largest electronics companies to stay home and help his two boys finish high school. Working at our company was his first job after they had graduated. And he had just given me a window into his soul. Now it all made sense.

The thing is, it took a long time to get to that place. I am definitely not suggesting that anyone should unnecessarily endure abuse or a harsh work environment. I knew I was supposed to be a part of that company. I knew God had called me to its people and its owner. Equipped with that revelation, I pressed into every relationship there.

I like to think my contribution to the organization made a difference somehow. I know what I got from it was a huge blessing to me and my family. Yet as I look back at that job and every job I have ever had, it's not the bottom line that I remember. It's the countless dinners shared. The moments traveling together. Being there for one another. Facing challenges and knowing that only together would we overcome them. I remember the people I loved, not the transactions we made.

Viktor E. Frankl said in *Man's Search for Meaning*, "For success, like happiness, cannot be pursued; it must ensue, and it only does so as the unintended side-effect of one's personal dedication to a cause greater than oneself or as the by-product of one's surrender to a person other than oneself. Happiness must happen, and the same holds for success: you have to let it happen by not caring about it."

Take that in: Happiness must happen. Your happiness isn't about you; you have to let go and let it happen to you. We find fulfillment only when we give ourselves in love to God and others. When God created you, he created you explicitly for this purpose. It is the only pursuit that will bring you true joy.

CHAPTER EIGHT

Bulletproof

"How blessed you are when you make peace! For then you will be recognized as a true child of God. 10 How enriched you are when you bear the wounds of being persecuted for doing what is right! For that is when you experience the realm of heaven's kingdom."
~ Matthew 5: 9-10

We demonstrate our capacity and willingness to love in our relationships—with God the Father and with others. So they are the ultimate measure of our success. But as everyone knows, relationships can also be quite difficult. Often we look to other measures of success to keep the ball on our side of the court: to maintain control. But love doesn't work that way. Control is the antithesis of relationship.[44]

So, as we dive into this topic, let's start by breaking down what a relationship actually is. If we define a relationship as "a mutual bond formed between two individuals," then we immediately find the challenge—other people. Their histories, their faults, their values, their quirks. We are built by God to desire, even need, relationships with family, friends, casual acquaintances, romantic partners. Each one is a chance to proactively love and be loved, and to feel disappointment, rejection, and pain. We all have experienced the full spectrum of relational successes and failures as we travel the highs and lows of loving others.

---

44 This is exactly what God did when he put the two trees in the garden. The ability to choose is what makes relationships real.

Past pain often causes us to walk timidly into the relational landscape around us, but it doesn't have to be that way. Look back at the verses beginning this chapter, Matthew 5:9,10 "9 "How blessed you are when you make peace! For then you will be recognized as a true child of God. 10 How enriched you are when you bear the wounds of being persecuted for doing what is right! For that is when you experience the realm of heaven's kingdom." When we read these verses in light of our relationship challenges, we see Jesus anticipated our pain. He has a blessing for you in His kingdom realm. In the Kingdom of God, our relationships can enter a new, protected space. It does not mean our experiences will be pain-free, but He does give us the promise of His healing, protection, and blessing.

It begins with understanding trust. We are born into this world full of trust, hardwired with the innate belief people are good and have our best interests at heart. In an ideal world, this instinct starts with our parents and extends to our siblings and close family. When we were hungry, they fed us. When we needed a clean diaper, they changed us. When we were frightened, they comforted us. Hour by hour, they proved themselves to be reliable and true.

Our earliest relational paradigm should be formed in the arms of nurturing parents. Scientists call this "bonding." It is the deep psychological connection between a newborn and his or her caregivers, and at its core is the concept of trust. We are literally programed to trust. The sight, sound, smell, feel of our parents is imprinted onto us.

One of my favorite memories as a young parent is letting our babies nap on my chest. It was as if the sound of my heartbeat and the warmth of our embrace had a magical effect on them. They would almost instantly relax and fall asleep.

All too soon it seems, children begin to learn the harsh reality that not everyone is trustworthy. Siblings take a favorite toy. Friends tease and poke fun on the playground. As a practical matter of safety, parents begin teaching us "don't go with strangers" and "don't run off in the store." Somewhere in our early formation we develop an internal trust-meter—an inner compass that directs our decision making. It begins like a binary switch: trust or don't trust.

But over time and through thousands of relational transactions, our trust-meter matures into a complex instrument sensitive to minute increments. We trust one friend more than another. We trust someone in one area of our life but not another. People regularly move up and down on our trust scale based upon our evaluation of their performance in our relationship.[45]

And then we introduce the issue of pain. Bullying. Embarrassment. Failure. The list is endless. Our relationships can become minefields. We extend trust only to have it betrayed. The betrayal hurts, so we withdraw. We learn. We heal. We extend again. We hit puberty and the emotions get wilder, and the knives get sharper. The cycle of trust-betrayal-hurt-heal-need-hope-try-trust repeats over and over, shaping our trust-meter with each iteration.

Beyond the day-to-day challenges, we have to factor in major life events. The death of a loved one, divorce, abandonment, a cross-country move, or a sudden shift in family economics can all cause a tremendous shock. By the time we enter adulthood, our trust-meter has evolved into a complex and sensitive system. All of our life experience has taught us one thing: Trust is earned! It's the only logical conclusion after years of trial and error, numerous points of pain, and countless relational interactions.

---

45 This is regularly demonstrated in the concept of adolescent "best friends." The jockeying back and forth to identify and connect with a BFF demonstrates the cycle of trust. We long to have a group of people we can be fully transparent with—a tribe we can identify with and find safety in.

But what if it's not true?

What if our fundamental assumption that trust is earned is simply wrong? What if we were hardwired correctly from the beginning? What if something in this broken world has introduced a virus into our system? What if our trust-meter is founded upon fear and not faith? And what if there is something we could do to change it?

Imagine with me a world where trust was innate, freely and often extended, even in our adult lives. Everything would be different! Our friendships, marriages, work relationships, family connections—everything!—would be dramatically altered. Our view of the world would shift. Our ability to find satisfaction in relationships would improve exponentially. Our fear of pain would melt away, and our boldness in extending ourselves would grow. All the energy we expend in self-protection could be directed toward loving others.

(Before we go too far, let me offer a disclaimer. We all experience relational pain and disappointment. That is a part of living. Abuse is something altogether different. If you are in relationships that are marked by cruelty, violence, or a pattern of demeaning behavior, speak up, get help, and get out. We have a phrase in West Texas that says, "Good fences make good neighbors." Trusting someone does not mean giving the free access to our hearts and lives. Setting clear boundaries helps us have healthy and successful relationships.[46])

Traditionally, relational trust is based upon our belief that someone is reliable, true, and safe. Our trust grows when others prove themselves to us, and it diminishes when they violate it.

---

46 A great book on this subject is *Boundaries Updated and Expanded Edition: When to Say Yes, How to Say No To Take Control of Your Life* by Henry Cloud and John Townsend.

The problem is that this depends entirely on our evaluation of another's behavior.

In many life instances, this "proven trust" is important. If I am looking for someone to care for my young children, I wouldn't just assume the best of a stranger—I'd ask my friends for recommendations and start with a few short outings. When I needed someone to repair my hernia, I selected my surgeon after checking out his credentials, history, and success rate—stuff that's way more important than bedside manner. When you're thinking about marrying someone, you need to date them long enough to get to know the "real" him or her.

When the real risk of failure is high, so is the need for proven trust. Yet for most of our relationships, the only real risk we face is getting our feelings hurt. Now, I am not minimizing the real pain caused by people who are close to us. I am suggesting that when our trust-meter is tuned to avoid pain, we force everyone to prove himself or herself before we are willing to trust them. Ironically, this can cause them to perceive us as withdrawn and untrustworthy ourselves.

Someone has to take the first step initiating the trust cycle by giving trust. I call this "gifted trust." By choosing to risk personal pain and disappointment, we can gift trust to others. Part of being a child of God is being willing to enter into risky situations of the heart, earn the genuine trust of others, and usher peace into their lives. When we gift trust we bring the relationship within the boundaries of the Kingdom of God.

The world is a difficult place. Wounded people with overly sensitive trust-meters are freely doling out rejection, sarcasm, and criticism to distract from their fear and pain. From the crass co-worker who seems to always tell the inappropriate joke to the class bully to the ultra-sensitive "emotional black hole," the people around us often broadcast pre-rejection as a protective mechanism.[47]

By now it won't surprise you to learn that Jesus upends this dynamic, suggesting that actually, our job is not to withdraw but to insert ourselves into these relational environments and bring peace. We do it by gifting trust, with healthy boundaries, to the individuals in our circles of influence. In a world built on relational quid pro quo, gifted trust is a rare commodity. Giving of oneself without expectation of reciprocity is the key to opening the locked hearts that surround us.

Gifted trust starts with God Himself. God created this world and put us in it. His only motivation was to have a family who could be in relationship with Him and with one another, but for it to be real He had to let us make the choice. Knowing we had the option to reject Him, and knowing many would, God still chose to go forward with His plan for humanity. He gifted trust to His beloved creation.

Jesus did the same. As he approached the last days of His life on earth, Jesus' opponents were looking for an opportunity to kill Him; however, His popularity with the people made it risky for them. Thus, they had to look for a time when he was in private to arrest Him. Jesus was aware of this, yet he longed to have a final Passover meal with His friends.

On the day the sacrifice of the Passover lambs was to take place, Jesus sent for Peter and John and instructed them, 'Go and prepare the Passover supper so we can eat it together.'

---

47 For a quick glance at the reality of this, watch any episode of "The Office" or "Parks and Recreation." Shows like these build their characters around the classic relational dysfunctions that occur around us daily.

They asked him, 'Where do we make the preparations to eat the meal?'

> *Jesus gave them this sign: 'When you enter [Jerusalem], you will find a man carrying a jug of water. Follow him home 11 and say to the owner of the house, 'The Teacher told us to ask you, 'Where is the room I may use to have the Passover meal with my disciples?' ' He will then take you to a large, fully furnished upstairs room. Make the preparations for us there.*[48]

This is a scene right out of a spy novel. Jesus sends His most trusted disciples—two of His closest friends—into the city. They were to look for a "man carrying a water pitcher." This would have been easy to spot, as fetching water was considered women's work in Jesus' day. A man carrying a water pitcher balanced on top of his head would have been easy to see in a crowd. And they were not to engage the man but to follow him. Once they saw which house the man went into, they were to approach the master of the house and utter the passphrase.

Clearly Jesus had gone to great lengths to keep the timing and location of this Passover meal a secret even from His dearest friends. Why? We find out toward the end of the meal. Let's continue with Luke: "After supper was over, he lifted the cup again and said, 'This cup is my blood of the new covenant I make with you, and it will be poured out soon for all of you. But I want you to know that the hands of the one who delivers me to be the sacrifice are with mine on the table this very moment.'"[49] There was a traitor in their midst! Judas had agreed to betray Jesus, and Jesus knew it!

And it gets worse. After dismissing Judas, Jesus leads His disciples to the Mount of Olives, their normal place of evening prayer.

"Along the way Jesus said to them, 'Before the night is over, you will all desert me. This will fulfill the prophecy of the Scripture that says: I will strike down the shepherd and all the sheep will scatter far and wide!'"[50] Ah, there's that image of the sheep again! Not only is Judas going to betray Jesus, but everyone else is going to completely abandon Him, too. And Jesus knows it! He knows His friends are going to abandon Him in His hour of greatest need. He knows that the sheep will run away. He even tells Peter that before the night is over, he will deny three times that he even knows Jesus.

So, what does Jesus do? As usual, He does the unexpected: He invites them to come even closer. "And he said to them, 'My heart is overwhelmed and crushed with grief. It feels as though I'm dying. Stay here and keep watch with me.'"[51] He gifted them trust with the full knowledge they would fail Him that very night.

Marvel's Wolverine is one of my favorite superheroes. It's not his claws or destructive nature I'm attracted to. It's his superpower. His body heals almost instantly from any cut, broken bone, or disease. He isn't necessarily bulletproof—he feels and experiences the agony of every shot, slash, and burn. But he instantly repairs himself. Essentially, he's indestructible.[52]

While this is clearly the stuff of comic books, spiritually we can live in such a way as to become relationally bulletproof. We can live above the distrust, backbiting, bullying, lying, and cruelty which crush so many relationships. It does not mean that the shots don't hurt. But living in the Kingdom of God means living in the presence of the King. And that means His healing power is available, 24/7, to repair our broken hearts.

---

50 Matthew 26:31
51 Matthew 26:38
52 Spoiler alert: I say "essentially" indestructible because as we all know he dies in *The Death of Wolverine* comic and as an adaptation of that story line, in the movie *Logan*.

The secret to activating this spiritual superpower is forgiveness. Jesus was very clear on the importance of forgiveness. In instructing his disciples in how to pray, Jesus says in Matthew 6:12: "[Father,] forgive us the wrongs we have done as we ourselves release forgiveness to those who have wronged us." He feels so strongly about this that he goes on to warn, "And when you pray, make sure you forgive the faults of others so that your Father in heaven will also forgive you. But if you withhold forgiveness from others, your Father withholds forgiveness from you."

We receive forgiveness from God, and God fully expects us to forgive others in turn. When we can learn how to forgive, we learn how to move quickly past the pain and back into peace. It makes us easy to love and makes loving others easier. When we are operating with active forgiveness in our lives, people are attracted to us because they can sense that we are safe. Instead of returning jab for jab, we counter with love. This does not mean that we don't stand up for ourselves. We are not to be punching bags for the world to beat up. It does mean, however, that our response is firm, but compassionate. We can defend without going on the offense.

To Jesus, forgiveness was like breathing. Out with the old, in with the new. Out with anger, envy, and strife. In with peace, harmony, and new life. Even as the Romans were nailing Him to the cross, He prayed, "Father, forgive them, for they don't know what they're doing."[53] In the midst of the pain and agony of torture, Jesus used His dying breath to ask God to forgive them. That is our standard, and that is the key to living bulletproof.

When we forgive, we release ourselves from the pain of the attack. Refusal to forgive holds *us*—not the attacker—in bondage. We may feel that if we do not harbor resentment for the people

---

who've wronged us, justice will never be served. We think we are somehow punishing the ones who wronged us, but in reality, we are punishing only ourselves. The attack hurts. No doubt. But it's the lingering resentment that infects us. When we refuse or are slow to forgive, we irritate the infection and the wound festers.

We won't find relationships that are completely immune to pain. There's no such thing. Even Jesus was betrayed by His friends! But thanks to Jesus we have the ability to rise above the pain.

When we embrace forgiveness, we gain the ability to gift trust. And gifting trust enables us to bring the Kingdom of God into every relationship. It is our calling. It is our purpose. It is our blessing.

In the words of Jesus in Matthew 5:10, "How enriched you are when you bear the wounds of being persecuted for doing what is right! For that is when you experience the realm of heaven's kingdom."

CHAPTER NINE

Pushing Through Life's Pain

Jesus answered them, "Give John this report: 'The blind see again, the
crippled walk, lepers are cured, the deaf hear, the dead are raised back
to life, and the poor and broken now hear of the hope of salvation!'
And tell John that the blessing of heaven comes upon those who never
lose their faith in me—no matter what happens!"
~ Matthew 11:4-7

We know by now that the Kingdom of God is the place where God rules and reigns. It is the place of blessing, provision, and empowerment. But at times, it is also a place of pain, disappointment, and frustration.

No honest discussion of the Kingdom of God would be complete without addressing the reality of human suffering. One of the most common questions people ask is: "If God is good, then why does he let bad things happen?" Philosophers and theologians have wrestled with this question throughout the ages, and I will leave the broader question to them. What I really want to address here is the more pressing—and practical—question of, "Why does God let bad things happen to me?"

Part of the answer lies in our power of choice. Remember those trees in the garden? God granted us free will. We can choose good or evil, to obey or rebel, to live in the Kingdom of God or to keep ourselves outside it. When we choose poorly, we should not be surprised when we run into the consequences of those choices. A very basic example: If I steal from my employer, it wouldn't be God's fault if I get fired.

But it isn't just you and me that have free will. Other people—billions of them—are out there making their own choices. Like it or not, when they choose poorly, we share in the consequences. The drunk driver speeding down the wrong side of the road and colliding head-on with a family is an all-too-common example of the power of someone else's choice affecting our lives. Suffering the consequences of another person's failure, whether it's intentional, accidental, or both, is the definition of tragedy.

Let's take the general example of mankind's impact on the environment. Regardless of where you stand on the environmental issues, it is clear God has granted to mankind a level of free will in choosing how we steward the natural world He created. The result of our collective choices forms a reality we each individually have to live with. It would be easy to say that the "good" things of our lives happen in the Kingdom of God and the "bad" things happen outside it. This logic allows us to neatly divide all our experiences into two buckets: a spiritually "blessed" bucket and a worldly "cursed" one. But if we dig just below the surface, we see that framework is hollow.

God is all knowing, all powerful, and ever present. If we pay attention, we will see His handiwork in our lives every day. He is not a dispassionate, distant King who sets the wheels of life in motion and then sits back to observe the drama play out. He plays an active part, guiding, interceding, and intervening as He shapes the course of our lives. (If I ever feel a doubt, I just remember my shooting star!)

Several months ago, my son and his fiancé were making the nine-hour drive home from college.[54] As they came into Decatur, just north of the Dallas Fort Worth metroplex, they stopped for a quick break. When they got back to the car, they noticed they had a flat tire. Forty frustrating minutes later, they were back on the road. Within fifteen minutes, they came upon a terrible wreck! First responders were actively working at the scene; clearly the accident had just happened. They both instantly recognized that the minor delay from the flat tire likely saved them from a much worse situation! God had intervened.

I believe this happens to us all the time. God directs and redirects our steps to prevent tragedy and present opportunities. He also directly inserts Himself to heal us, strengthen us, and empower us. So, the ultimate fallacy with the "two-bucket logic" is this: If God can intervene, but chooses not to, then He is ultimately responsible for the outcome. He is to "blame."[55]

In the late fall of 2011, our family received some shocking news. My father, who had been having some headaches, suddenly passed out at home. Thankfully, the medics were able to revive him. My mom loaded him into the car and drove ninety minutes to the VA hospital in Amarillo, where he was diagnosed with glioblastoma multiforme (GBM), an aggressive brain cancer. Within twenty-four hours, he was airlifted to the VA hospital in Albuquerque, which was better equipped to perform the delicate brain surgery he urgently needed.

We were all stunned by the speed at which everything was happening. I googled GBM to get an idea of what we were dealing with. The results were not encouraging. Doctors and scientists don't

---

54 Now his beautiful wife!

55 I say "blame" not because He has done something wrong. He cannot do wrong as He is the very definition of right. But as we'll see a bit later on, it is our view of God's action vs. inaction when we are in pain that causes us to want to lay the responsibility at His feet—often in the form of accusation against our King.

'BM; there are no clear genetic markers or life-
ct it. It is a rare disease that seems to strike at
ig they were certain about was the prognosis.
~...y survived twelve to fifteen months with aggressive
treatment and fewer than three months without. Dad choose to
fight it, believing—as we all did—that God can work miracles if we
give Him a chance.

But we didn't get a miracle. After a brutal fifteen months, Dad
succumbed to the disease and went home to be with his beloved
Lord. He was only sixty-five years old.

When the pain we are facing is deep, almost paralyzing, it is
much more difficult to accept simple answers like "It was just his
time" or "God was ready for him to be in heaven" or "These things
just happen sometimes." I get it; we can't explain why. I really appreciated the encouragement people offered as we grieved, but in that
moment, the explanations all fell flat. Dad loved God and had spent
his life serving Him. Why did he get this disease? He did not deserve
it. Why didn't God heal him? I know God to be a healer. Is GBM too
big for Him? Does He not care? Were my prayers not enough?

In his wonderful book, *A Grief Observed*, C. S. Lewis described
his struggle with these doubts after the loss of his wife. He says,

> *Meanwhile, where is God? ... When you are happy, so happy that*
> *you have no sense of needing Him, so happy that you are tempt-*
> *ed to feel His claims upon you as an interruption, if you remem-*
> *ber yourself and turn to Him with gratitude and praise, you will*
> *be—or so it feels—welcomed with open arms. But to go Him*
> *when your need is desperate, when all other help is vain, and*

what do you find? A door slammed in your face, and a soun‹
bolting and double bolting on the inside. After that, silence.[56]

In other words, it's easy to believe in God and feel His love when things are good. But when life is painful, and loss is real, it's tempting to believe that God shut the door on us. That He doesn't care. That He isn't going to help us in our hour of need. Lewis goes on to say,

Not that I am (I think) in much danger of ceasing to believe in God.
The real danger is of coming to believe such dreadful things about
Him. The conclusion I dread is not 'So there's not a God after all,'
but 'So this is what God's really like. Deceive yourself no longer.'[57]

When we are faced with tragedy, crisis, or even simple disappointment, we want someone to answer the question, "Who's to blame for this?" If we can apportion blame, we can assign responsibility and exact vengeance. But when the finger points toward God, what are we to do? Instinctively, we know blaming God is wrong, but the question pounding in our hearts is "why?" Why would You let this happen? Why didn't You do something? Why don't You care? Why can't You see how much I'm suffering, and do something about it? Why!

The answer is exceedingly simple, yet excruciatingly difficult: Surrender. We simply submit. We let go of trying to answer the question of "why" altogether. We stop demanding an explanation. We release all judgment. This is easier said than done—but once we do it, we experience tremendous freedom and healing.

---

56 Lewis, C.S.: *A Grief Observed.* HarperCollins e-books, page 17.
57 Ibid.

I've had several occasions with God where I found myself up against this very paradox. I knew Him to be good, but my pain seemed too much for a good God to put me through. During one such occasion while I was wrestling with God, I heard Him say, "My son, it's not that I am withholding the 'why' from you. You are simply not equipped to understand it." Just because I didn't know what God was doing didn't mean that God didn't know what He was doing.

God spoke to the prophet Isaiah, saying, "'My thoughts are nothing like your thoughts,' says the Lord. 'And my ways are far beyond anything you could imagine. For just as the heavens are higher than the earth, so my ways are higher than your ways and my thoughts higher than your thoughts.'"[58]

All the whys belong to the King. And in the Kingdom of God there is only room for one King. The throne is occupied. What we find in these moments is that our demand for an answer to why is really a challenge for His throne—at least as it relates to our specific situation. We know better. We would have done things differently. We want a different outcome.

We struggle to see the difference between a Kingdom and a democracy. Yet it is in these times of difficulty—the moments when our will is pitted against the will of God—that we experience the difference. My good friend Pastor Jimmy Evans once said, "You don't know if someone is truly submitted until their will is crossed." It's hard to let go. It's hard to say "your will be done" instead of "my will be done." But He is in charge. He makes the call. We don't get a vote. Letting go of the why is terrifying, but also liberating. When we surrender to the King's will—even if we will never understand it—we land firmly in the Kingdom of God.

---

58 Isaiah 55:8,9 (NLT)

The Bible supplies us with an incredible example of this paradox in John the Baptist, the forerunner to Jesus and His ministry. He was Jesus's cousin and friend, a great leader, teacher, and prophet who stood up for righteousness. In Matthew chapter 11, we find John in jail. John had been publicly critical of Herod—the Roman leader over the region—for stealing his brother's wife.

When John hears that Jesus is nearby, he sends his disciples to ask Jesus a question. "Are you the savior we've been expecting, or should we be looking for someone else?" Now that was a loaded question! John has spent his entire life preparing the way for Jesus. They are family. He no doubt heard the story of how Jesus was conceived and born. He knew about all the miracles Jesus performed. He of all people knew who Jesus was. So, why ask Him this question?

If we read between the lines a little, I think we can see what John is really asking: "Hey cuz! If you haven't noticed, I'm in jail here. If you don't do something quick, I'm going to be executed. Now would be a great time to do your 'Messiah thing,' overthrow the Roman government, and get me out of here! Will you please help me?"

Jesus's answer was both compassionate and clear. "Give John this report: 'The blind see again, the crippled walk, lepers are cured, the deaf hear, the dead are raised back to life, and the poor and broken now hear of the hope of salvation!' And tell John, 'Blessed are those who are not offended over me—no matter what happens!'"[59]

The list of miracles was a specific one—blind, crippled, lepers, deaf, dead—all healed. These were all the miracles listed in the book of Isaiah that the Messiah was prophesied to perform.[60] John surely

59 Matthew 11:4-6
60 Isaiah 29:18-19; 35:5-6

would have known this. Jesus shares another thing the Messiah was foretold to do: rescue the poor and brokenhearted. Here Jesus is referencing the prophet Isaiah: "The Spirit of the Sovereign Lord is upon me, for the Lord has anointed me to bring good news to the poor. He has sent me to comfort the brokenhearted and to proclaim that captives will be released and prisoners will be freed."[61]

Wait a minute! Jesus only quoted the first half of this passage. In his response to John, he replaced the "captives will be released and prisoners will be freed" with "blessed are those who are not offended over me—no matter what happens!" This was Jesus transmitting a direct message to John. He was telling John, "My friend. I am the Messiah. You know this. I'm choosing to leave you in prison to die. There is a blessing for you if you choose not to be offended with me over this."

John was beheaded not long after this.

"Blessed are those who are not offended over me." How hard it is for us not to be offended! But how much grace there is to be found in God's kingdom! It is a blessing to relinquish control and responsibility to the King. The only alternative is to carry the responsibility and bear the burden on our own, and we simply are not equipped to manage it. So, we have to learn to let go. To give up on our demand for explanations. To release our judgments and blame. To stop trying to balance the equation ourselves.

Submitting to the King is not passive. It's not a last resort. It's an active choice.

When we choose not to be offended by our King and His decisions, on the other side of our pain, disappointment, and anger, we find our Father. He may not offer specific answers, but He freely gives His compassion, love, and grace. We choose—moment by

---

moment—to trust in His goodness even when we can't see it for ourselves. We choose to lean in to the dark night of the soul. And as we reach madly for the only anchor we know, we find our God, our rock and sanctuary. And we find ourselves deeper in the Kingdom of God than we have ever traveled before.

CHAPTER TEN

Lighting Up the World

"Your lives light up the world. Let others see your light from a distance, for how can you hide a city that stands on a hilltop? And who would light a lamp and then hide it in an obscure place? Instead, it's placed where everyone in the house can benefit from its light. So don't hide your light! Let it shine brightly before others, so that the commendable things you do will shine as light upon them, and then they will give their praise to your Father in heaven."

~ Matthew 5:14-16

We live in the Kingdom of God, and the Kingdom of God lives in us. We have the privilege of experiencing the blessings of the Kingdom and the responsibility to share those blessings with the world. As Christians, each one of us has Jesus literally living within us. The Apostle Paul shares in Romans 8:10, "Now Christ lives his life in you!" This is an incredible truth! The Kingdom of God is both a fixed, spiritual place and a mobile, internal reality that accompanies us everywhere we go.

When our bodies give up their last breath here on Earth, we take our next breath in Heaven, our eternal home. In the meantime, we are citizens on a journey in a foreign land. We live in the world—and because and we carry the Kingdom of God with us, we can influence the world with God's goodness.

Several years ago, I was on a business trip with Paul, my UK-based European Sales Manager. We were making the three-and-a-half-hour drive from Vienna, Austria to Prague, Czechia.

We also had a Czechian salesman with us. As we approached the Austrian border, Paul pulled our car over at the checkpoint to show our passports to the border patrol agent. I watched as he put my U.S. passport on top of the pile. The agent took all three passports, opened mine, looked at my picture, matched it to my face sitting in the passenger seat, and waved us through. He never even looked at the other two passports.

At the Czechian border, about one hundred meters down the road, Paul switched the order, putting my passport on the bottom of the pile and our Czech friend's on top. Again, the Czech border patrol agent looked only at the top passport, matched the face with our friend in the back seat, and we were waved through. I was blown away by the whole process!

I asked Paul about the passport order switch. "The Austrians," he explained, "love the Americans. The Czechs? Not as much. By putting your passport on top, we gained favor with the Austrians. And by putting the Czech passport on top we gained favor with them." In that moment I fully experienced the importance of citizenship. In a real sense, I was recognized not for who I am individually—Jimmy Witcher—but by the country to whom I belong: a citizen of the United States of America. There was real, tangible power in that belonging!

A U.S. passport is an incredible document. It gives American citizens permission to freely leave and return to the United States. And it also gives us direct access into many countries without having to apply for permission ahead of time. If we run into trouble in a foreign land, the U.S. State Department will step in and assist us. Our citizenship allows us to carry the freedom we enjoy at home out into the world.

Regardless of our physical place of birth, you and I are citizens of the Kingdom of God, and the Holy Spirit is our spiritual passport. Ephesians 1:13 tells us, "Now we have been stamped with the seal of the promised Holy Spirit." You are an earthly ambassador for the Kingdom of God. You bring the freedom and authority of being a child of God and citizen of the Kingdom of God with you everywhere you go. Think of all the places you've been this past week: the office, coffee shop, gym, church, restaurants, your kids' soccer games, school, home. The Kingdom of God went with you everywhere!

Peter says it this way in 1 Peter 2:9-10, "you are God's chosen treasure—priests who are kings, a spiritual 'nation' set apart as God's devoted ones. He called you out of darkness to experience his marvelous light, and now he claims you as his very own. He did this so that you would broadcast his glorious wonders throughout the world. 10 For at one time you were not God's people, but now you are. At one time you knew nothing of God's mercy, because you hadn't received it yet, but now you are drenched with it!"

Recognizing how this spiritual reality impacts our practical, day-to-day activities is critical. Once we begin to recognize we carry the authority of our heavenly passport with us, the question becomes, "What do we do with it?"

We've talked a lot about how we each have a unique purpose and journey. But I believe that no matter how our paths differ, we are all called primarily to do two things with our citizenship authority: First, we are called to expand the influence of the Kingdom of God. And second, we are called to help others find and enter it. As citizens of the Kingdom and subjects of the King, we are charged with using our gifts, abilities, and energy to increase God's influence on the world. That happens every time a citizen of heaven takes a leadership position, exerts their influence, or stands up for what is right. It happens every time we take the opportunity to let others in on the blessing of living in the Kingdom of God. This is more than our sovereign right and responsibility: it's also the best deal in the universe!

Jesus preached in His Sermon on the Mount, "Let others see your light from a distance, for how can you hide a city that stands on a hilltop?" There is a town in Galilee, Tz'fat, that sits atop a hill on the northwest corner of the Sea of Galilee. It's likely that Jesus referring to this town; everyone would have understood the reference. After dark, the city lights were a beacon, providing a sense of direction like a lighthouse. Fishermen and travelers looked to it for navigation.

What a beautiful metaphor Jesus gives us. We are to shine like Tz'fat. But how? What does that mean in our modern lives? First and foremost, we do our very best where God has us stationed right here and now. One of the great lies we tell ourselves is what I call the lie of "one day." One day I will conquer this bad habit. One day I will find the right person to marry. One day I will have a position of real influence. Only then can I change the world.

Friends, that day is today. You already have a circle of influence! God has given it you, whether it's school, work, home, or in your community. When you invest where you are on this day, God is always faithful to expand your reach.

Don't believe the lie our modern culture tells us about the importance of separating religion from every other sphere of life. We are encouraged to keep our spiritual and secular expressions of ourselves apart. What we do at church is distinct from what we do at school or work or with our friends. Our religious beliefs are to be private, internalized—not expressed outside of church. Put simply, this is crazy. It's like going into a fight with an arm and a leg tied behind your back.

Now, I am not saying we should stand on our desks and shout scripture to our coworkers. That's not being a light—that's being a nuisance! We are way more likely to turn people off instead of inviting them in. But there are a million ways we can bring the Kingdom of God into every room, decision, and activity that we are a part of—because the Kingdom of God is in us. Where we go, it goes!

Let me share an example. Early in my business career, our company decided to try our hand in another market. I was assigned to work with an outside consultant named Jim to develop our business plan, product line, and launch model. We spent months together grinding out the details of the new business. And as we went through, I found myself getting lost in the accounting details.

I went to school to be a chemist, not a businessperson. The only business class I ever took was a programming class. I began to pray for understanding. One night I had a dream. I saw a prism—like the one you used in elementary science class to make rainbows—drop down in front of my view. A profit and loss statement appeared and stuck to one side, then a balance sheet on another, and finally a cash flow statement on the third. Then I zoomed inside the prism, and saw connections being made between the three reports. Instantly, I understood how they all worked together! It seemed that God had supernaturally downloaded what I needed to learn to put the business plan together.

Jesus told His disciples in John 14:26, "But when the Father sends the Spirit of Holiness, the One like me who sets you free, he will teach you all things in my name." The Holy Spirit is here to teach us all things: math, science, relationships, leadership, accounting, sales, marketing, parenting—everything! I'm not saying everything will be transmitted in a dream. That's only happened once for me. But, we can read, study, and learn to become an expert at anything because we have the Holy Spirit. It is part of our inheritance in the Kingdom of God. As we apply our learning with diligence, we become a real asset wherever God has placed us, and we can answer His call to shine our light in the darkness.

The business venture we tried ultimately failed. We greatly underestimated the time it takes to break into a new market. But the impact this learning experience gave me was huge! It became the framework for many opportunities we were able to capitalize on later. The process was a crucial step in me gaining greater influence and opportunity in the organization. As the Kingdom of God made the way for me, I gained more opportunities to carry the Kingdom of God with me—even to places of tremendous darkness.[62]

Las Vegas has never been one of my favorite cities, but as the leading trade show site in the country, it was unavoidable. Every year we had at least one and often two or three corporate trade shows there. That was where our business was conducted so that was where I needed to be. My role in the organization meant I would be hosting clients every evening. Inevitably, someone—a client or coworker—would say after dinner, "We are all going to the strip club. Want to come?" My answer was always the same: "No thanks, I'm tired and need to get up early in the morning. I'll catch you guys later."

Over time, my colleagues noticed that I never participated. When they asked why, I would tell them the truth: "I'm happily married to my best friend. That's not my kind of thing." Next thing you know, the two of us would be sitting down in the hotel lobby

---

62 Shortly after this experience, Jim commented to me, "Man, you have a good understanding of business. Where did you get your business degree?" I responded, "I don't have one, but God showed all of this to me one night. It suddenly all made sense." Jim just stared at me for a second, then went on like I did not say a thing. I've always wondered what he really thought of that encounter.

bar discussing their marriage struggles. I'd share with them stories about how Kim and I have struggled in the past, and how only with God's help and grace we made it through to the other side.

Notice the difference: I wasn't judging their situation, condemning their choices, or disavowing them. But neither was I conceding that their response was okay. By not judging but remaining true, I had a platform to share the light of the Kingdom of God with them. Those were some of my favorite moments in business.

As citizens in the Kingdom of God, we should work hard at our jobs, serving our employers with every gift we have. We should be diligent at school, investing the time and energy needed to be successful. We should serve and love the people in our circles: our families, our friends, our neighbors. We should ask God to help us on this day, and we should draw upon the resources of the Kingdom of God with full trust that he will multiply them in all our efforts.

As citizens of the Kingdom of God, we have an unfair advantage—one that I am completely delighted to tap into. We have access to the blessings of God. We have the Holy Spirit living inside of us. We can draw upon Heaven's creativity, empowerment, and knowledge for every activity we participate in.

We shine by carrying the Kingdom of God with us in our endeavors, and we shine by sharing its benefits with others. Paul shares in 2 Corinthians 5:20, "We are ambassadors of the Anointed One who carry the message of Christ to the world, as though God were tenderly pleading with them directly through our lips. So we tenderly plead with you on Christ's behalf, 'Turn back to God and be reconciled to him.'"

Ambassadors play a powerful role: they represent and speak for their leader. Just as the U.S. Ambassador to France can address the French President on behalf of the President of the United States, as ambassadors for Christ, we represent Christ to others. We are a "stand in," giving them a glimpse—however imperfect—into who Jesus is. This is not about being preachy and it's certainly not about being judgmental.

Think about Jesus and His approach. Jesus simply lived with people and freely shared how much God loved them. He was and is a model of holiness and perfect ambassador for the Father. Jesus was the absolute balance of Spirit and truth. He held the perfect standard; yet constantly extended grace and mercy to those who fell short.

Lighting up the world is about being transparent, accepting, yet still resolute about living in truth. It's about investing everything you have into the tasks that God has put in front of you. It's about drawing upon the resources of the Kingdom of God you have available to you. Above all, it is about loving one another—loving them so much that you both refuse to judge them and refuse to leave them alone in their pain and struggle. The Kingdom of God is at hand, and we can show them the way. This is, after all, Jesus's last commandment!